Exploring Teachers' Pedagogical Choices in Using Textbooks to Teach English

"This is an engaging presentation of the specific case of language textbook use and development in Mauritius. The authors do an excellent job of contextualizing the study locally while also situating it in the broader international landscape. I particularly appreciate that the teachers' voices come through clearly. The volume will be welcomed by those interested in textbook development, curriculum and teacher training."

—Rita Elaine Silver, Associate Professor, *Emeritus National Institute of Education, Nanyang Technological University*, Singapore

Yesha Devi Mahadeo
Rajendra Korlapu-Bungaree
Komal Reshma Gungapersand
Mangala Jawaheer

Exploring Teachers' Pedagogical Choices in Using Textbooks to Teach English

Curricular Reform and Minority Textbook Writers' Agency in Mauritius

Yesha Devi Mahadeo
Mauritius Institute of Education
Reduit, Mauritius

Rajendra Korlapu-Bungaree
Mauritius Institute of Education
Reduit, Mauritius

Komal Reshma Gungapersand
Mauritius Institute of Education
Reduit, Mauritius

Mangala Jawaheer
Mauritius Institute of Education
Reduit, Mauritius

ISBN 978-3-031-98538-6   ISBN 978-3-031-98539-3 (eBook)
https://doi.org/10.1007/978-3-031-98539-3

© The Editor(s) (if applicable) and The Author(s), under exclusive license to Springer Nature Switzerland AG 2025

This work is subject to copyright. All rights are solely and exclusively licensed by the Publisher, whether the whole or part of the material is concerned, specifically the rights of translation, reprinting, reuse of illustrations, recitation, broadcasting, reproduction on microfilms or in any other physical way, and transmission or information storage and retrieval, electronic adaptation, computer software, or by similar or dissimilar methodology now known or hereafter developed.
The use of general descriptive names, registered names, trademarks, service marks, etc. in this publication does not imply, even in the absence of a specific statement, that such names are exempt from the relevant protective laws and regulations and therefore free for general use.
The publisher, the authors and the editors are safe to assume that the advice and information in this book are believed to be true and accurate at the date of publication. Neither the publisher nor the authors or the editors give a warranty, expressed or implied, with respect to the material contained herein or for any errors or omissions that may have been made. The publisher remains neutral with regard to jurisdictional claims in published maps and institutional affiliations.

Cover illustration: Pattern © Melisa Hasan

This Palgrave Macmillan imprint is published by the registered company Springer Nature Switzerland AG.
The registered company address is: Gewerbestrasse 11, 6330 Cham, Switzerland

If disposing of this product, please recycle the paper.

Preface

This book represents our journey as minority textbook writers and teacher educators, as we engage with the complexities of textbook implementation in the Mauritian secondary school system. It reflects our commitment to understanding teacher's pedagogical choices when using the textbooks we designed, conceptualised and wrote, recognising that textbooks are not merely static objects, but dynamic tools shaped by the hands and minds of minority textbook writers as well as teachers.

Through in-depth analysis of case studies, we explore the real-world classrooms of English language teachers, reflecting on how they perceive, adapt, reimagine (and even bypass) the MIE textbooks. We, then, discuss the dissonance between minority textbook writers' cognition and agency pitted against teacher cognition and agency, highlighting the challenges and opportunities of any major curriculum reform in Small Island Developing States [SIDS], such as Mauritius.

This book represents an invitation to dialogue and a call for collaboration between minority textbook writers, teacher trainers and teachers themselves. It is a reminder that textbooks are not merely ends in themselves but rather means to empower teachers and inspire students on their journey of learning and textbook writing is a iterative, complex process that demands further research.

Reduit, Mauritius	Yesha Devi Mahadeo
Reduit, Mauritius	Rajendra Korlapu-Bungaree
Reduit, Mauritius	Komal Reshma Gungapersand
Reduit, Mauritius	Mangala Jawaheer

Acknowledgements

We would like to express our sincere gratitude to the teachers who participated in this study, allowed us access to their classrooms and shared their experiences and insights with us. They were eager to engage in open and honest dialogues, and their stories have provided us with a deeper understanding and appreciation of textbook implementation and teacher agency in the Mauritian context.

We acknowledge the complex realities of teachers and learners who engage with the intricacies of textbook and curriculum implementation daily. We hope that sharing our findings with a broader audience will offer an insight into how teachers take ownership of their pedagogical practices in the face of curricular reform. We also want to acknowledge our own experiences, as **minority textbook writers**, which interwove with the fabric of this book, rendering a deeper insight to the findings that we share with our broader audience. We aim at engaging different stakeholders of curricular reform in the reflection of how challenging it is to conceptualise, design and write government-endorsed textbooks, as minority textbook writers. We hope that this book provides an insight into how curricular reform, as a process is complex and the importance of having different stakeholders engage collaboratively to lead to the enactment of any reform.

Finally, we are also grateful to the Mauritius Institute of Education (MIE) for funding and supporting the research that fed into the writing of this book.

Competing Interests The authors have no competing interests to declare that are relevant to the content of this manuscript.

Contents

1 **Setting the Scene** 1
   1.1 Introduction 2
   1.2 Structure of This Book 2
   1.3 Textbook Research and Situating Minority Textbook Writers 3
   1.4 Government-Endorsed and Approved School Textbooks 4
   1.5 Multilingual Landscape of Mauritius 5
   1.6 The Mauritian Multilingual Educational System 6
   1.7 The Major Educational Reform of the NYCBE (2016) 7
   1.8 The NYCBE and the Need for Government-Mandated Textbooks 8
   1.9 Process of Writing the Government-Endorsed English Textbooks in Mauritius 8
   1.10 Minority English Textbook Writers: An Act of Reclaimed Agency? 9
   1.11 Conclusion 10
   References 10

2 **The Place of the Textbook in a Curricular Reform** 13
   2.1 Introduction 13
   2.2 Global Trends in Curricular Reform 14
   2.3 The Textbook: The Cogwheel in Curricular Reform 16
   2.4 The Teacher: The Driver of a Curricular Reform 18

	2.5	Teacher Cognition and Agency: The Engine of Curricular Reform	20
		References	23
3	**Planning and Implementing the Study**	27
	3.1	Orientation to the Chapter	27
	3.2	Research Design and Approach	28
	3.3	Selection of Participants	30
	3.4	Generating Data	32
	3.5	Data Analysis	36
	3.6	Ensuring Trustworthiness and Credibility	37
	3.7	Limitations	37
	3.8	Conclusion	38
		References	38
4	**The Voices of the Drivers of Curricular Reform**	41
	4.1	Orientation to the Chapter	41
	4.2	Reema: The Ace Driver	42
	4.3	Vedi: The Obedient Driver	51
	4.4	Pranav: The Entitled Driver	56
	4.5	Rabiah: The Defensive Driver	61
		References	70
5	**Curricular Reform in a SIDS: Teacher Cognition and Teacher Agency Locking the Brakes to Curricular Reform**	71
	5.1	Orientation	71
	5.2	Teacher Cognition: Teachers' Perceptions of Government-Endorsed English Textbooks	72
	5.3	Teacher Agency: Teachers' Pedagogical Choices When Using the Government-Endorsed Textbooks	77
		Reference	83
6	**Minority Textbook Writers' Cognition and Agency**	85
		References	91

Concluding Thoughts	93
Curriculum Change and Teacher Agency	94
References	97
Index	105

About the Authors

Yesha Devi Mahadeo-Doorgakant is a lecturer in the English Department at the Mauritius Institute of Education (MIE), Mauritius. She is specialised in Educational linguistics and holds a PhD from the University of KwaZuluNatal. Her publications explore multilingual educational systems as well as multilingual practices of learners in Mauritius. Her professional work as lecturer is majorly geared towards developing teachers' skills and competencies to teach English in the multilingual context of Mauritius. She is also engaged in curriculum development at primary as well as secondary level. She was entrusted with the responsibility to pioneer the conceptualisation, design and writing of the secondary Grades 8-9 English/English literature textbooks. She was a visiting researcher and lecturer at Harvard University, USA in 2024–2025. Her research interests include multilingualism, translanguaging and multilingual pedagogies used within multilingual educational systems as well as a range of qualitative methodologies such as ethnography, narrative inquiry and collaborative autoethnography. She also writes short stories which have been published in the *Collection de Maurice* editions.

Rajendra Korlapu-Bungaree is a senior lecturer in the English Department at the Mauritius Institute of Education (MIE), Mauritius. His academic interests include language and literature teaching methodologies, media in education, values and citizenship education and human rights education. He has been involved in projects pertaining to the implementation of communicative language teaching strategies at both primary and secondary level, and communities of practice in academic settings. His research interests are centred around English language and literature pedagogies, literature didactics, academic well-being, teacher agency and teacher decision-making.

Komal Reshma Gungapersand is a senior lecturer in the English Department at the Mauritius Institute of Education (MIE), Mauritius. She is specialised in applied linguistics and special education needs. She has taught in Mauritius and in the UK. She holds a Master's Degree in International ELT and Applied Language Studies from London Metropolitan University, UK. She also holds a Postgraduate Diploma in Inclusive and Special Education and a Master's Degree in Comparative Education. She worked as a teacher and assistant teacher in the Special Educational Needs (SEN) Department in different schools in the UK. She is involved in curriculum development at different levels at the Mauritius Institute of Education. She is a Certified Trainer in Inclusive Education. She is enrolled on an Education Doctoral programme with the University of Brighton, UK. Her research interests include ethics education, dialogic teaching, applied linguistics, comparative education, inclusive and special education. She has written research papers in international journals. She believes that teaching is an ongoing transformative process.

Mangala Jawaheer is Lecturer in English at the Mauritius Institute of Education (MIE), Mauritius. Her main interests revolve around pedagogical approaches in English language teaching and literature teaching. She is currently pursuing her doctoral studies at University College London, UK, and her focus is on the pedagogical content knowledge of teachers for the teaching of literature at secondary level.

Abbreviations

MIE	Mauritius Institute of Education
NCE	National Certificate of Education
NCF	National Curriculum Framework
NCF-S	National Curriculum Framework-Secondary
NYCBE	Nine Years' Continuous Basic Education
TLS	Teaching and Learning Syllabus

List of Figures

Fig. 2.1 The mechanism of curricular reform   15
Fig. 6.1 Curricular reform and the pull direction   89

List of Tables

Table 3.1	Participants' profile	31
Table 3.2	Number of interviews for each participant	32
Table 3.3	Total number of observations	33

CHAPTER 1

Setting the Scene

Abstract The expository chapter sets the scene for a qualitative, longitudinal empirical study on teachers' perceptions and pedagogical choices when using the government-endorsed Grades 7–9 English textbooks in Mauritius, which were conceptualised, designed and written in the context of the NYCBE curricular reform. It discusses the conceptualisation, design and writing of government-endorsed secondary textbooks to provide a thick description of the context underpinning this study. Drawing from Das' notion of subaltern perspectives (Das, 2023), this chapter takes a step further by positioning the authors as subaltern' English textbook writers, renamed minority textbook writers in this book, who have reclaimed their voice, agency and cognition as textbook writers, functioning within the parameters of a Small Island Developing State country as Mauritius.

Keywords The textbook • Curricular reform • English textbook writing and government endorsed textbooks • Subaltern perspectives/ Minority textbook writers • Reclaimed agency • In-service teachers' perceptions • Pedagogical choices

1.1 Introduction

It is not a presupposition that most of us, as students, have used school textbooks at least once in our school life. If we go back in time and think carefully, hopefully, we will remember one textbook that held some meaning for us. There may be multifarious reasons why there are memories of this textbook. It could be that we had an affinity or dislike for the textbook as students and it will give us an insight into how we viewed the textbook as being part of our learning experiences.

As teachers or academics, it is very likely that we have referred to or used a particular textbook at least once in our careers. We may have stumbled upon it when researching for our classes or courses or it may have been part of our faculty's prescribed reading list. We may have used this textbook in various ways. For instance, we may have used it for exploratory or explanatory reasons, for practice exercises or to draw inspiration to create our own. We may have used the textbook in segments or from beginning to end. Albeit the different reasons that we might have for using a textbook, at that point in time we made a conscious decision to use it as a resource for our teaching, and it might have helped shape or refine our teaching, becoming part of our teaching toolbox. If we delve a bit deeper, we may argue that we chose this particular textbook because it satisfied our notion of quality, and it was somehow related to our teaching ideology. In this book, we thus hope to contribute to existing scholarship on textbook evaluation where we look at how teachers' perceptions and pedagogical choices influence their use of government-endorsed English language textbooks at secondary level. Its key contribution is that it provides an insight into in-service teachers' perceptions and pedagogical choices of government-endorsed textbooks during the implementation of a curricular reform and how they reject curricular reform at grassroot level. It also extends the discussion to the reflection that pans out from the perspective of those who conceptualised, designed and wrote these government-endorsed textbooks and attempts at filling the gap in existing knowledge on this field of study.

1.2 Structure of This Book

This book is divided into several chapters. This chapter purviews the literature on textbook research and sets the scene for this longitudinal qualitative study. It proceeds to delineate the conceptualisation, design and writing of government-based secondary textbooks whilst providing a more holistic and nuanced description of the context underpinning this study. This chapter goes a step further by positioning the authors as minority English textbook writers who have reclaimed their agency before introducing readers to the rationale for this study and the research focus. Chapter 2 surveys extant scholarship on the writing of the English language textbook, teacher beliefs and their agency in using or rejecting the textbooks. It also opens the scope on research on the field of minority textbook writers and their cognition as well as agency. Chapter 3 underlines the methodology for this longitudinal qualitative study. Chapter 4 presents the core findings of the research carried out and the analysis from these findings is fleshed out in-depth in Chap. 5. Chapter 6 discusses these analytical elements pertaining to textbook writing literature and problematises the position of the minority English textbook writers.

1.3 Textbook Research and Situating Minority Textbook Writers

As textbooks are valuable resources for teaching in educational systems (Khan et al., 2024), textbook scholarship is a dynamic and multidisciplinary arena, branching into diverse and at times overlapping strands (Bock, 2018). Focal areas include textbooks, theorisation and methodology; textbooks linked to a discipline and school teaching (Bock, 2018); textbook design, procedures and processes; the use and adaptation of textbooks by teachers; textbook evaluation (Khan et al., 2024); textbooks as cultural and historical educational artefacts (Kumar, 2023); textbooks and technology (Bruillard, 2021); and textbooks and digitisation (Bock, 2018). According to Johnsen (1993), textbook research gained formalisation and momentum in the 1990s as several countries (Austria, Germany, Japan and Sweden) set up separate institutions for scholarship in this field. Three decades later, textbook research is now an established field of study. This comes as no surprise as textbooks continue to play a critical role in educational systems despite the upsurgence of digitisation and easy availability of resources on the Internet (Mahboob & Elyas, 2014; Bruillard, 2021; Bock, 2018).

Textbook writers are a motley batch. For instance, there are freelance textbook writers with experience and subject expertise who respond to calls from local and international educational publishing houses. Often, these textbook writers are teachers with considerable experience. They may work in silos or with other teachers. There is another group of textbook writers who are renowned scholars in a particular discipline and are solicited by reputable international educational publishing houses as their work brings credibility. They often undertake textbook writing to contribute to the discipline. Research in this area focuses on whether publishing houses revise and replace textbooks that align with specific curricular reform demands (Bakken & Andersson-Bakken, 2021).

On the sideline, there is a minority group of textbook writers who write textbooks for entirely different reasons. These textbook writers are experienced academics with subject expertise who work under the aegis of a particular government. As per the mandate of the higher education institution they are affiliated to and employed by, they are required to produce curriculum-related materials and government-endorsed textbooks to meet national curricular reform. In short, they are called upon to write textbooks as part of their professional duties. Interestingly, they do not collaborate with educational publishing houses.

These textbook writers often wear multiple hats. They are academics, teacher trainers, curriculum developers and textbook writers who are keenly aware of the need for textbook alignment with curricular reform. In other words, they understand the referential and programmatic function of the textbook as the practical interpretation of the official programmes (Bruillard, 2021) as they have been involved in the process of curricular reform. Referring to English language textbook writing, Atkinson (2021) underscores how these textbook writers have adaptive expertise to transfer their subject expertise of English language teaching and teacher training to the domain of textbook writing. For the purpose of this book, we are will be referring to this group of textbook writers as *minority textbook writers*.[1] This will, in turn, fill the existing gap on minority textbook writers as a field of research.

1.4 Government-Endorsed and Approved School Textbooks

Although textbook writers writing for government-endorsed textbooks exist in several countries, the contexts differ. For example, in Saudi Arabia, the Ministry oversees the content of English textbooks to ensure that local religious and cultural norms and traditions are respected (Mahboob &

---

[1] Our emphasis.

Elyas, 2014). In the same vein, in Pakistan, the Federal Directorate of Education controls the production of English textbooks (Khan et al., 2024). Although there is existing literature on textbook writing, qualitative scholarship on minority textbook writers' experiences, working on government-endorsed textbooks, is *relatively scant*.[2] Arguably, it seems that this group of textbook writers is often left on the periphery, especially since their roles and reasons for writing textbooks are different from textbook writers, producing textbooks in different contexts.

In this optic, this chapter is two-pronged. Primarily, its key function is to present an in-depth insight into the context of this book. It presents a situational description of Mauritius, an overview of its educational system and a reflection on the recent curricular reform which led to the conceptualisation, designing and writing of government-mandated textbooks. It proceeds to overview the processes and procedures of writing government-endorsed textbooks in Mauritius. Its secondary purpose is to respond to the gap in scholarship on textbook writers from Small Island Developing States (SIDS) who are mandated to produce government-endorsed textbooks and build a case for their voices to be heard. Essentially, it gives space for the often-untold experiences of a particular group of English language textbook writers and the reasons for embarking on qualitative textbook research.

1.5   MULTILINGUAL LANDSCAPE OF MAURITIUS

The Republic of Mauritius is a small island developing state (SIDS) situated in the Indian Ocean with a population of approximately 222 thousand and is considered as a pioneer in Sub-Saharan Africa (Schwab, 2019). Due to its rich colonial history, Mauritius presents a complex linguistic landscape. After being discovered by the Arabs and visited by the Portuguese and Dutch, it is a double colony, having been successively colonised by the French and the British. Though the island gained independence from the British in 1968, the imprint of the colonisers on its linguistic and education landscape still prevails: Mauritian Kreol, a language that emanated from slavery,[3] is spoken by over 86.5% Mauritians

---

[2] Our emphasis.
[3] "Mauritian Creole has emerged as the lingua franca among slaves who were forced to interact in a common language with other slaves from other tribes sharing a different linguistic code, as well as with the French colonizers" (Nadal et al., 2017, p. 206).

(Central Intelligence Agency, 2020). French, perceived as the language of prestige, is commonly used in social and formal spheres though it is the home language of only 4.1% Mauritians; English, which is spoken by less than 1% Mauritians and is often viewed as a foreign language, occupies a privileged status as the language of parliament as well as the medium of instruction in schools. Ancestral languages (ALs)[4]—such as Hindi, Tamil, Telugu, Urdu and Modern Chinese—and Arabic also pepper the language ecology. Upon admission to a primary school, the young Mauritian child is taught English and French, and an optional AL or Arabic. Since 2012, Mauritian Kreol is also included in the list of ALs that the child can choose from (Nadal & Ankiah-Gangadeen, 2018). Other core subjects at this level include Mathematics, Science, and History and Geography. All these subjects, except for French and optional languages, are taught in English. At secondary level, the spectrum of subjects taught widens but the same linguistic policy prevails since the language-in-education policy is still determined by the colonial document, the Education Ordinance 1944 (Colony of Mauritius, 1957). Whether this situation denotes a parochial clinging on to colonial vestiges or the pressures of neo-colonial forces that propel small island developing states (SIDS) like Mauritius to adapt to the global world (Phillipson & Skutnabb-Kangas, 2009), it has resulted into daily challenges within the field of teaching and learning with most learners across the island being taught in a complex multilingual educational system. The difficulties are exacerbated by the fact that the highly competitive national examinations held by the local examining body (the Mauritius Examinations Syndicate) at the end of the primary cycle, and the foreign examination body (the University of Cambridge) at O and A Levels, are in English.

1.6 The Mauritian Multilingual Educational System

There have been multiple educational reforms post-independence. Education in Mauritius was decreed free for primary and secondary levels in 1976 and for tertiary level in 2019 (Bunwaree, 1994). Secondary education is divided into two levels: lower and upper secondary. Lower secondary comprises Grades 7 to 9 and culminates in the National Certificate

---

[4] The term 'Ancestral Languages' is used to refer to languages that were spoken by the Mauritian forefathers who immigrated or were brought to the island during the colonial era.

of Education examinations (NCE). Upper secondary comprises of Grades 10–13. These culminate to the Cambridge School Certificate and the Cambridge Higher School Certificate Examinations. A failure in English for the Cambridge School Certificate equates to an automatic failure for learners. It must be pointed out that the practice of taking into account the linguistic profile of diverse learners for instructional purposes dates as far back as the colonial times, as seen in the Education Ordinance (1957)—which replicates the Education Ordinance dated 1944:

> In the lower classes of Government and aided primary schools up to and including Standard III, any one language may be employed as the medium of instruction, being a language which in the opinion of the Minister is most suitable for the pupils.
>
> In Standards IV, V, and VI of the Government and aided primary schools, the medium of instruction shall be English, and the conversation between the teacher and pupils shall be in English; provided that lessons in any other language taught in the school shall be carried on through the medium of that language. (Colony of Mauritius, 1957, pp. 129–130)

However, while the Ordinance advocates switching to English as medium of instruction as from Standard IV,[5] it should be brought out that Mauritian Kreol and/or French have been used at all levels as languages used to scaffold the teaching of English in the multilingual classrooms of Mauritius.

1.7 The Major Educational Reform of the NYCBE (2016)

The Nine Year Continuous Basic Education (NYCBE) is an educational Mauritian curricular reform aligned with the UN Sustainable Development Goal 4 to "ensure inclusive and equitable quality education for one and all and to promote lifelong learning" (Ministry of Education and Human Resources Tertiary and Scientific Research, 2016, p. 5). This reform is founded upon "6 pillars: Curriculum Change, Innovative Pedagogies, Meaningful Assessment, Continuous Professional Development, Conducive Learning Environment, and System Governance and Accountability" (Ministry of Education and Human Resources Tertiary

---

[5] The new appellation, following the NYCBE reform, is Grade 4.

and Scientific Research, 2016, p. 9). The stated aim of the NYCBE (MIE, 2016) is to create an internationally competitive workforce where all young Mauritians have equal and equitable access to inclusive education. The NYCBE reform (MIE, 2016) has led to several educational policy decisions: (1) The Special Education Needs Authority Act; (2) The Scholarships to Children from Vulnerable Families; (3) Digital Youth Engagement Programme and (4) Free Higher Education in Public Tertiary Education Institutions. Under this reform, students follow nine years of basic education with the choice of choosing vocational or academic subjects for Grade 10.

1.8 The NYCBE and the Need for Government-Mandated Textbooks

The Mauritius Institute of Education (MIE) was commissioned to produce the National Curriculum Framework (NCF, 2016), the Teaching and Learning Syllabus (TLS, 2016) and to conceptualise and design government-endorsed textbooks across primary as well as lower secondary level, which was a pioneering first for academics working at the Mauritius Institute of Education. As the textbooks were an essential wheel on the curricular reform, there was an urgency for the textbooks to be conceptualised, designed and written nationwide so that they could be used in government and confessional primary and secondary schools at the beginning of the academic year.

1.9 Process of Writing the Government-Endorsed English Textbooks in Mauritius

The conceptualisation, design and writing of the Grade 7-9 English textbooks was underpinned by the philosophy governing the NYCBE reform, the NCF (MIE, 2016) and the TLS (MIE, 2016). As the panel leaders and several panel members were academics[6] who had conceptualised the NCF and TLS, they were able to ensure curriculum coherence (Oates, 2014) by mapping the textbooks upon the conceptual framework of the TLS, focusing on the development of skills, competencies and attitudes. Engaged in ongoing research, they also had a deep understanding of the multilingual

---

[6] Responsible for empowering teachers teaching at different levels in the country as well as writing textbooks at secondary level.

educational landscape and the position of English within this context. Hence, using their adaptative skills in teacher training, their subject-specific expertise in English language teaching and their understanding of the multilingual educational landscape and the position of English within this context, they designed the lower secondary textbooks with a focus on using learner-centred and skills-based approaches (Atkinson, 2021). A content-based approach and drill exercises for examination preparation were not included as these did not match the philosophy governing the NYCBE reform as well as the NCF and TLS which were the crucial documents governing this curricular reform (MIE, 2016).

Following the implementation of the NYCBE reform through the conceptualisation, design and writing of the government-endorsed English textbooks, we conducted a qualitative, longitudinal study that spun out the research which is feeding the writing of this book. Setting up the context as well as highlighting the intricacies of the process of textbook writing allows us to better understand the perspectives of minority textbook writers conceptualising, designing and writing government-endorsed books and offers a critical analysis into what a challenging process textbook writing can be in such a paradigmatic reality.

1.10 MINORITY ENGLISH TEXTBOOK WRITERS: AN ACT OF RECLAIMED AGENCY?

In the backdrop of Das' (2004) notion of subaltern perspectives, we, the authors of this book, consider ourselves to be four 'subaltern', *minority textbook writers* who have decided to reclaim our agentic power through several actions. Drawing on the literature on teachers as change agents of curricular reform (Humes & Priestley, 2021) and their own professional beliefs about the importance of the voices of teachers, we engaged in a longitudinal qualitative study to look at the pedagogical choices made by in-service teachers in using the government-endorsed textbooks that we have conceptualised, designed and written. Curriculum literature points to teachers as key actors in the implementation of curriculum change as their agency can be located on a continuum spanning from acceptance to resistance (Janko & Pešková, 2017). Craig posits that teachers have the agency to activate curricular reform in their pedagogical choices to meet the specific needs of their students in their micro-context (Craig, 2009).

Smith (2006) argues that the perceptions and use of school textbooks by in-service teachers are implicitly connected to curricular reform. In the context of Mauritius, in-service teachers' perceptions of and engagement with government-endorsed textbook is an integral part of curricular reform, yet perusal of the local scholarship indicates that there is a gap that exists in textbook scholarship. Reporting on the perceptions, pedagogical choices and practices of in-service teachers using government-endorsed English textbooks will shed a practical and theoretical dimension to better understand the complex process of textbook writing when it is mandated for a curricular reform and will situate minority textbook writing as a research area. Moreover, it will also fill the existing gap on minority textbook writers' scholarship.

1.11 Conclusion

This introductory chapter has described the contextual reality of textbook writing of academics who write government-endorsed textbooks at national level, following the major NYCBE curricular reform in Mauritius. It has situated the philosophies governing the position of these minority textbook writers who are viewed as being as 'subalterns' and a backdrop in this curricular reform, when they are responsible for bringing into reality the curricular reform by driving the conceptualisation, designing and writing of the key philosophical documents, like the NCF (National Curriculum Framework) and the TLS (Teaching and Learning Syllabus) and the textbook which we refer to as the cogwheel of curricular reform, for the purpose of this book.

References

Atkinson, D. (2021). The adaptive expertise of expert ELT textbook writers. *RELC Journal, 52*(3), 603–617.

Auleear Owodally, A. M. (2014). Socialized into multilingualism: A case study of a Mauritian pre-school. In J. Conteh & G. Meier (Eds.), *The multilingual turn in languages education: Opportunities and challenges* (New perspectives on language and education) (pp. 17–40). Multilingual Matters.

Bakken, J., & Andersson-Bakken, E. (2021). The textbook task as a genre. *Journal of Curriculum Studies, 53*(6), 729–748. https://doi.org/10.1080/00220272.2021.1929499

Bock, A. (2018). Theories and methods of textbook studies. In E. Fuchs & A. Bock (Eds.), *The Palgrave handbook of textbook studies* (pp. 57–70). Palgrave Macmillan.

Bruillard, E. (2021). *Textbooks: current research and practices, some markers.* Retrieved July, 27, 2024. https://gis2if.org/wp-content/uploads/2021/04/Bruillard-textbooks_research.pdf

Bunwaree, S. (1994). *Mauritian education in a global economy.* Editions de l'Océan Indien Ltée.

Central Intelligence Agency. (2020). *The world factbook: Africa-Mauritius.* https://www.cia.gov/library/publications/the-world-factbook/geos/mp.html

Colony of Mauritius. *The Education Ordinance. 1957. A collection of ordinances proclamations and government notices published during the year 1957.* (1958). J. Eliel Felix, I.S.O., Government printer.

Craig, C. J. (2009). Research in the midst of organized school reform: Versions of teacher community in tension. *American Educational Research Journal, 46*(2), 598–619. https://doi.org/10.3102/0002831208330213

Humes, W., & Priestley, M. (2021). Curriculum reform in Scottish education: Discourse, narrative and enactment. In *Curriculum making in Europe: Policy and practice within and across diverse contexts* (pp. 175–198). Emerald Publishing Limited.

Janko, T., & Pešková, K. (2017). Exploring teachers' perceptions of curriculum change and their use of textbooks during its implementation. A review of current research. *Zeitschrift für Geographiedidaktik \ Journal of Geography Education, 45*(1), 33–60. https://doi.org/10.18452/23097

Johnsen, E. B. (1993). *Textbooks in the kaleidoscope.* Oxford University Press.

Khan, A., Rafique, S., & Khalid, S. (2024). Evaluation of the Federal English textbook of Grade One of Federal schools in Pakistan. *Journal of Applied Linguistics and TESOL (JALT), 7*(4), 70–84.

Kumar, K. (2023). *Textbooks and the curriculum: Understanding the politics.* Retrieved from [chrome-extension://efaidnbmnnnibpcajpcglclefindmkaj/ [https://www.thehinducentre.com/the-arena/67053469-Textbooks-and-the-Curriculum-Understanding-the-Politics.pdf] (chrome-extension://efaidnbmnnnibpcajpcglclefindmkaj/ [https://www.thehinducentre.com/the-arena/67053469-Textbooks-and-the-Curriculum-Understanding-the-Politics.pdf] (https://www.thehinducentre.com/the-arena/67053469-Textbooks-and-the-Curriculum-Understanding-the-Politics.pdf))

Mahboob, A., & Elyas, T. (2014). English in the kingdom of Saudi Arabia. *World Englishes, 33*(1), 128–142.

Mauritius Examinations Syndicate. (2015). *Mauritius—National assessment at Form III.* http://nada.uis.unesco.org/nada/en/index.php/catalogue/175

Mauritius Institute of Education. (2016). *National curriculum framework: Nine-year continuous basic education Grades 7, 8 & 9*. http://fliphtml5.com/eisr/sgym/basic

Mauritius Institute of Education. (2018). *Curriculum*. https://portal.mie.ac.mu/curriculum-development/

Ministry of Education and Human Resources Tertiary and Scientific Research. (2016). *Nine years of continuous basic education: Inspiring every child*. http://ministry-education.govmu.org/English/educationsector/nys/Documents/NYCBE%20Booklet.pdf

Nadal, P., & Ankiah-Gangadeen, A. (2018). Parental choice in the learning of Mauritian Kreol at school: The motivational factors. *African Perspectives of Research in Teaching and Learning*, 2(1), 64–87.

Nadal, P., Ankiah-Gangadeen, A., & Kee Mew, E. (2017). Navigating between outward-looking socioeconomic aspirations and inward-looking international education drives for SIDS: Can Mauritius sail out of cross-currents? In J. Tavis & P. Ressler (Eds.), *Is 'small' always small and 'big' always big? Re-reading educational policy and practice in small states*. Peter Lang.

Oates, T. (2014). *Why textbooks count a policy paper*. University of Cambridge, Local Examinations Syndicate.

Phillipson, R., & Skutnabb-Kangas, T. (2009). *The politics and policies of language and language teaching*. The handbook of language teaching, 26–41.

Schwab, K. (2019). *The global competitiveness report 2019*. http://www3.weforum.org/docs/WEF_TheGlobalCompetitivenessReport2019.pdf

Smith, A. (2006). Education for diversity: Investing in systemic change through curriculum, textbooks, and teachers. In E. Roberts-Schweitzer, V. Greaney, & K. Duer (Eds.), *Promoting social cohesion through education: Case studies and tools for using textbooks curricula* (pp. 29–46). The World Bank.

CHAPTER 2

The Place of the Textbook in a Curricular Reform

Abstract This chapter delves into the existing literature on curriculum design, textbook use and teacher agency, setting the theoretical foundation for the study. It explores the importance of textbooks in language teaching, especially in the context of reformed curricula. The chapter also examines the role of teacher cognition, beliefs and pedagogical choices in textbook implementation.

Keywords Textbook and the teacher • Reformed curriculum • Teacher cognition • Pedagogical choices • Teacher agency • Exam-oriented approach • Challenges

2.1 Introduction

In this chapter, we reviewed thoroughly the research that was carried out on how textbooks were an essential element of curricular reform in varying international contexts, surveiling closely the use of English language textbooks in such contexts. We found that there is a dearth of research carried out on how ***minority textbook writers conceptualised, designed and wrote textbooks to implement curricular reform***. Moreover, locally, no research has been carried out to explore how the major NYCBE curricular reform, which necessitated the conceptualising, designing and writing of Grade 7-9 secondary English textbooks, was received by English

© The Author(s), under exclusive license to Springer Nature Switzerland AG 2025
Y. D. Mahadeo et al., *Exploring Teachers' Pedagogical Choices in Using Textbooks to Teach English*,
https://doi.org/10.1007/978-3-031-98539-3_2

language teachers, in Mauritius. We, thus, had to move to reviewing literature in international contexts to be able to draw a deeper analysis on how ***minority textbook writers*** wade their way through the different elements of curricular reform, thereby filling the gap in the existing literature. In this chapter, therefore, we considered studies from different multilingual contexts on textbooks and curriculum change and the perceptions of teachers on English language textbooks as well as the challenges they faced while using the textbooks. Studies pertaining to English teachers' agency, their cognition and how this, in turn, informs their beliefs towards curricular reform were also reviewed to better understand the pedagogical choices made by teachers when using the textbooks designed to teach English in Mauritius. Following this, we were better able to come up with an analytical frame for the findings emanating from the study conducted; findings which we lay out in this book. ***We, thus, view the government-endorsed textbooks as being a minor cogwheel within curricular reform as we view the teachers as being the drivers of curricular reform, with their teacher cognition and agency acting as engines, gearing their pedagogical choices*** (see Fig. 2.1). Our findings will, therefore be analysed against this theoretical backdrop, which emanated from the literature reviewed and this will guide our understanding of what direction teacher cognition and agency give to curricular reform.

2.2 Global Trends in Curricular Reform

Driven by the evolving needs of the twenty-first century, there has been a surge in curricular reform which has resulted in materials and resources being changed globally. The curriculum in any educational system defines what content needs to be taught and how it should be taught. Curricular reform can be enacted in manifold ways. Curricular reform is a global trend which endeavours to deliver curricula focused on meeting the challenges and needs of the twenty-first century where knowledge is seen as specific subject facts, learned through transmission by a teacher (Mitchell & Buntic, 2023). Curricular reform in many countries is synonymous with improving the quality of education, shifting from content-based to outcomes-based curricula, hence laying emphasis on the development of skills, attitudes and values in any curriculum. This shift meant that there were more curriculums advocating for learner-centred pedagogies (Ibid.).

However, curriculum change is not always enacted positively. Kim (2024) criticises the fact that teachers do not change while the curriculum

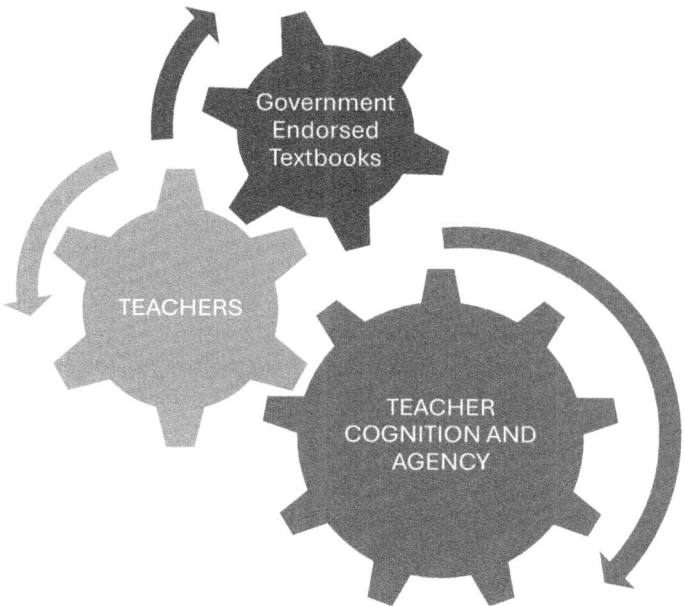

Fig. 2.1 The mechanism of curricular reform

keeps changing and that teachers' negative reactions to curricular reforms are widespread in many countries around the world. He asserts the fact that there is 'hidden' resistance and opposition on the part of teachers in the centralised education system of South Korea. Even in countries such as Finland, the 2016 curricular reforms met with resistance from teachers (Sahlberg, 2021). From the research done, we have gleaned that teachers do not welcome national curriculum revisions because it entails the change in content as well as methods of teaching (Kim, 2024). After perusal of studies conducted on curricular reform which offers the landscape to the research that we conducted, we feel it is of utmost importance to look at curricular reform from the perspective of **minority textbook writers** due to the fact that we are grounded in this contextual reality, mapped out already in Chapter One. In so doing, we seek to explore how textbook writers, as us, can navigate the current curricular reform to handle the dissonance that arises from our philosophies guiding the revised national curriculum and the teachers' resistance against any curricular change. *It is* *important to understand how teachers enact the curriculum through the new curriculum materials conceptualised and written to handle any future curricular reform better, design contextually appropriate textbooks whilst still maintaining agency as minority textbook writers.*

2.3 The Textbook: The Cogwheel in Curricular Reform

For the purpose of the audience of this book, we feel that it is highly significant to define what is meant by 'a textbook'. According to Hornby et al. (2000), a textbook is a book that is used in schools or colleges to teach a specific subject. Moreover, **a textbook can be understood to be one of the resources, if not the main resource, for teaching and learning.** Prescribed English textbooks for Grades 7 to 9[1] in the Mauritian context are written by academics,[2] who are employed by Mauritius Institute of Education and who also wear the hat of curriculum developers/designers and minority textbook writers **as well as teacher educators who train teachers of all levels.** These textbooks have been designed according to the Teaching and Learning Syllabus (TLS) (MIE, 2017) for Grades 7 to 9. The TLS for English provides the content of what is to be taught, and the knowledge, skills, competencies, attitudes and values that need to be developed and is an important document that guides the philosophy of the Nine Year Continuous Basic Education Reform (NYCBE).

The TLS, which articulates the learning outcomes for each Grade, **serves as a road map for the design of textbooks focusing on the use of the skills-based as well as the process approach.** Hence, the textbooks connect the NYCBE (MIE, 2016) and the TLS (MIE, 2017), putting a lot of emphasis on developing students' skills, competencies, attitude and behaviour. As such, the English textbooks for Grades 7 to 9 have been carefully organised in units designed to develop the different English language skills; namely communication skills, reading as well as writing, with grammar and vocabulary integrated within the teaching of these skills.

English textbooks play a crucial role in the teaching of English in multilingual contexts since they provide learning experiences stipulated in the designated multilingual curriculum. Nunan (1999) propounds that the English textbook is considered as the major resource to present

---

[1] Lower secondary in Mauritius.
[2] Academics who work at Mauritius Institute of Education.

knowledge and information in an organised way. This idea is seconded by Carranza and Cuayahuitl (2015) who expound that officially prescribed textbooks are helpful since they provide teachers with guidance in the planning of lessons and lesson materials which is in line with the espoused curriculum. Parlindungan et al. (2018) assert that in the multilingual context of Indonesia, locally published English textbooks play a pivotal role in developing linguistic and cultural knowledge of English at middle school level (equivalent to Grades 7 to 9 which is lower secondary level in Mauritius). In Japan and Korea where English is not required in daily talk, the textbook is a tool which is oriented towards developing specific as prescribed in the curriculum. For example, in the comparative study by Yuasa (2010), the textbook is used in Korea to develop students' speaking skills in the target language, while in Japan, textbooks are catered to arouse learners' interests in the foreign culture to help reinforce their communicative competence. It can be noted that when there is a curricular reform, textbooks serve as a means to an end. They lead towards curricular change, should they be enacted in the classroom as per the vision of educational stakeholders. This was indeed the philosophy that guided the English curricular change in Mauritius as the English language textbook has been specially conceptualised, designed and written within the framework of the NYCBE reform and translates the learning outcomes mapped out in the revised NCF (MIE, 2016) and the related TLS (MIE, 2017).

This aligns with suggestions by both international and local scholars who claim that locally produced textbooks are important because they have the possibility of considering the local cultural and contextual realities which might be overlooked by imported English textbooks and allow for the enactment of curricular change. Kumaravadivelu (2006) argues that authorial ownership of textbooks should be given to local experts who are knowledgeable about the culture, needs and local realities. In the context of curriculum reform sought by the NYCBE, the English textbooks were considered to be very important resources that would drive curricular reform. Hence, the minority textbook writers firmly believed that the newly designed English textbooks would bring about change from a grammar-centric language teaching to a skills-based teaching, therefore leading to better reception by learners across the different grades. In this vein, teachers were expected to enact this curricular reform using the government-endorsed textbooks, moving from a teacher-centred and grammar-centric approach to a more learner-centred and skills-based approach. Our purpose in the study that we conducted was to inform ourselves of the pedagogical choices made by the teachers when using the textbooks that we had conceptualised, designed and written. We also had a multipronged aim at understanding our own philosophies as ***minority textbook writers*** for any future reform that we might be engaged in and how to flesh out our own skills at conceptualising, designing and writing textbooks that lessen the dissonance between the government's philosophy and the teachers' strong philosophic stance towards the teaching of English.

2.4 The Teacher: The Driver of a Curricular Reform

Curricular reform entails new approaches to the teaching of English as well as revisiting textbooks from a different perspective. Reformed curricula have triggered numerous research studies on the teaching of English in multilingual contexts. Our literature draws on research done in multiple contexts, including Asian as well as Middle East contexts. Such studies investigate the effectiveness of the curriculum while highlighting teachers' cognition and practices based on the reformed curriculum. A study on the reformed curriculum in Vietnam found that teachers used their existing deep-rooted knowledge and beliefs about English language teaching and learning to enact the reformed curriculum in their own ways (Tran et al., 2023). The study concluded that Vietnamese teachers had a strong teacher agency and that their practice was informed by their teacher cognition. This view is supported by Nguyen (2014) who found that English teachers' enactment of the curriculum in the Vietnamese context was largely drawn from their knowledge and beliefs.

However, curricular reform might present some challenges in the teaching of English in multilingual contexts. Factors such as learners' poor English proficiency, time constraint, classroom management issues disparity between curriculum objectives and assessment practices have been cited as being some of hindrances to the teaching of English in Hong Kong (Carless, 2007). Teaching of English in Mauritius, whether with the former curriculum or with the reformed curriculum, has often been seen as being exam-oriented (Mahadeo, 2006; van Steen, 2019), hence widening the gap between the objectives of the reformed curriculum and assessment. Datnow (2020) argues that issues of agency and power influence the role of teachers in various waves of reform while Li et al. (2021) argue that English teachers' openness towards English language curricular reform and teacher professional development are among the factors which impact implementation at school. Teachers' receptivity towards curriculum changes influences how they interpret and translate reform policies in their classroom practices (Wallace & Priestley, 2011).

In other multilingual contexts, studies conducted on the perception(s) of English teachers on English language textbooks provide useful insight into the nature of existing textbooks whether locally produced or imported. Many teachers suggest the necessity of adapting the materials to suit the needs of their learners. In a similar vein, Tosun (2013) claimed that English teachers in Turkey found that the English textbook that was commonly used in Turkish schools failed to satisfy teachers' expectations since their teaching experiences and techniques varied. He, further, asserted that although the English textbook was an effective teaching tool in the hands of a good teacher, adopting a foreign textbook required a thorough needs analysis and rested on the competence of the teacher to be able to adapt to suit the needs of learners. In Thailand, Srakang (2013) found that English teachers who were pro textbook believed that without the textbook they would not be able to teach effectively while some teachers believed the textbooks needed to be supplemented by other materials to suit the needs of learners. On the contrary, Srakang (2013) also found that anti-textbook teachers perceived the textbooks as being ineffective and this hugely affected their use of the textbook. Rosyida (2016) found that teachers did not always follow all the prescribed sequences of the materials and activities suggested by the textbook author, but that their perceptions are influenced by some factors like personal experience, students' ability needs and interests, situation, workshop/training.

English teachers' perceptions on new English textbooks reveal that despite changes in the new textbooks, teachers found the content to be unsatisfactory and, hence, believed that new textbooks needed to be reviewed again (Ebrahimi & Sahragard, 2017). Khan et al. (2020) analysed the perceptions of English teachers in Pakistan, on English textbooks at secondary school level and found that teachers did not have a thorough knowledge of the textbooks. Although most of the teachers acknowledged that the textbook covered all language skills, they were uncertain about whether the textbooks comprised activities to improve students' language skills. In the light of such findings, it is crucial to understand English teachers' perceptions of the government endorsed English secondary textbook in Mauritius, the teachers being a cogwheel of the curricular reform in Mauritius, as stated before in Chapter One.

Several scholars (Rahimi & Hassani, 2012; Uysal & Bardakci, 2014) focus on teachers' views and beliefs on the suitability of the content. A study by Ahour et al. (2014) in Iran reveals that teachers believe that the content of the textbooks is irrelevant to the needs, interests and concerns of students. In the same vein, Uysal and Bardakci (2014) highlight how teachers prefer imported textbooks as they believe that these are more relevant and interesting compared to local ones. This is substantiated by Rahimi and Hassani (2012) who underscore the importance of revising the content of local textbooks in selecting relevant and engaging topics/materials to motivate learners to develop their language competencies. Other studies indicate that prescribed textbooks are not level-appropriate (Carranza & Cuayahuitl, 2015; Latif & Mahmoud, 2012; Rahman et al., 2019; Underwood, 2012). Latif and Mahmoud (2012) stress that teachers feel that curriculum designers are unaware of the proficiency level of students, which impacts on an appropriate pitching of textbooks. Okoth (2016) posits, in his study of Kenyan teachers' perceptions of prescribed textbook, that teachers believe that these textbooks are complex and overloaded with inappropriate details and information not aligned to the contextual reality and interests of learners. Keeping the different research done on teachers' resistance to enact the English language teaching curricular reform as backdrop, our research further expounds on how we, as ***minority textbook writers, situate ourselves in the face of the dissonance, resistance, push and pull contextual reality that we continuously find ourselves in,*** **due to our deeply ingrained learner-centric philosophy which clashes with the teachers' exam-centric philosophies**.

2.5 Teacher Cognition and Agency: The Engine of Curricular Reform

Scholarship in ELT is a multipronged nexus of study. One branch of ELT focuses on how teachers learn to "integrate and organise content of a textbook to make learning an interactive and meaningful experience" rather than using the textbook as a form of self-directed study (Wen-Cheng et al., 2011, p. 91). Haß (2006) expounds that the way EFL textbooks are used depends on multiple factors with the teacher being deemed the most important. According to Borg (2003), ***teacher cognition refers to what*** *teachers know, believe and think about teaching* and how these impact their daily practice. Existing literature therefore indicates that when teachers believe that the materials in the textbooks are unsuitable, they feel the need to compensate by adapting existing materials or supplementing the content with additional or diverse types of materials (Carranza & Cuayahuiltl, 2015). Furthermore, the time factor is indeed an important consideration in the implementation of activities as this inhibits the optimal development of learners' language competencies (Carranza & Cuayahuiltl, 2015; Ghorbani, 2011; Latif & Mahmoud, 2012; Panezai & Channa, 2017; Raees, 2018; Underwood, 2012). Literature reveals that teachers' perceptions of prescribed textbooks impinge on whether they use textbooks and if they do, the ways in which they use them (Raees, 2018; Uysal & Bardakci, 2014). Several studies (Raees, 2018; Rahman et al., 2019) indicate that teachers do not embrace textbooks **when they do not believe in the approaches or do not perceive the affordances of specific approaches that have been used** and thus resort to traditional teacher-centred ways of teaching English.

As mentioned above, one of the reasons for adhering to such beliefs can be accounted to teacher cognition (Raees, 2018; Rahman et al., 2019; Panezai & Channa, 2017) which cannot be dissociated from *teacher agency*. Jenkins (2020) asserts that *one aspect of teacher agency is when teachers try to control or influence the curriculum according to their beliefs*. For example, proactive teacher agency is when teachers act on their personal motivation which may not be aligned to any curricular reform (Ibid.). If teachers believe that their current teaching approach best suits their learners, they will not necessarily embrace other approaches that textbooks introduce them to. Yakavets et al. (2023) assert that there is limited evidence that teachers in Kazakhstan embraced sustainable ways of changing their teaching practice. The study indicates that only a surface change occurred in the teachers' beliefs and pedagogical practices. Teachers may continue to use traditional approaches if they have not received or if they think or believe that they have not received adequate training in using the new textbooks (Okoth, 2016; Rahman et al., 2019; Underwood, 2012). In such cases, they will continue to use traditional language approaches which are most familiar to them and with which they are more comfortable.

In the context of this study, it is crucial to consider a broad definition of teacher agency as an inner capacity (Bandura, 2006) based on notions of pedagogy, personal beliefs and principles or as actions. One such action is the implementation of the English textbook at school. Teacher agency is also influenced by professional development in the context of school reform (Imants & Van der Wal, 2020). Appadoo-Ramsamy (2022) asserts that those English teachers in Mauritius who are always challenging the relevance of reforms or questioning standardisation processes such as imposed textbooks are complex individuals whose agencies are always evolving. Teachers' reactions to curriculum should not be taken at face value especially by policymakers since they are the main drivers of any curricular reform. This complexity is highlighted in Korlapu-Bungaree's (2020) study, where English teachers in Mauritius exercised their agency in their choice of pedagogies of risk and safety, sometimes choosing to enact more conservative (and thus, safer) pedagogical actions in their classrooms in the face of a strong accountability and exam-driven school culture.

This literature review acknowledges the importance of teacher agency in the implementation of any curricular reform and attitudes towards the use of the new textbooks. However, research indicates that there is an existing gap on the beliefs of curriculum designers as well as minority textbook writers when it comes to conceptualising, designing and writing textbooks. Hence, this study takes a step further by shifting the perspective towards their stance as well as agency taken during this major curricular reform.

2.5.1 Exams: The Licence Shaping Teacher Cognition and Agency and Informing Their Pedagogical Choices and Teaching

In multilingual contexts, studies show that textbooks are mostly exploited for exam practice and less for accentuating the authentic experiences of learners when developing their English language skills. Lee and Bathmaker (2007) found that in the Singaporean context, in schools where students were less academically inclined, teachers were greatly influenced by targeted pass rates and used the textbooks for exam preparation This resonates with the exam-oriented Mauritian educational system characterised by 'rat race' competition (Jinot, 2017) which moulds language teaching and shapes teachers' exam-centric teaching philosophy.

A recurrent finding in the literature reveals that assessment is very often *the* major deterrent which impacts on teachers' implementation of prescribed textbooks and any curricular reform. On the one hand, Latif and Mahmoud's (2012) study indicates that many teachers tend to be exam-oriented and prefer to concentrate on the teaching of grammar, vocabulary, reading and writing, to the detriment of speaking and listening skills as these are usually not formally assessed. On the other hand, over-reliance on the prescribed English textbooks results in exam-oriented, teacher-centred pedagogies and exam-centric teaching philosophies (Latif & Mahmoud, 2012). This resonates with a study conducted with trainee teachers in Mauritius on their perceptions of constructivism as a pedagogy to teach literature in English at lower secondary level which showed that teachers made a conscious choice to be teacher-centred and exam-oriented in their practice (Jawaheer, 2019). Furthermore, Jawaheer puts forth that the textbook was the only resource that these teachers had at hand and she states that analysis of prescribed texts at lower secondary level is often dictated by the upper secondary syllabi and examination (Jawaheer, 2022). In some cases, teachers feel the pressure of the washback effect and prefer to concentrate on teaching for assessment rather than using the prescribed textbooks to develop language skills holistically.

This literature, therefore, offered the adequate theoretical backdrop against which we read and analysed the findings that emanated from the study we conducted on the use of government-endorsed books by teacher, in the light of the new curricular reform and allowed us to better position our own cognition and agency as *minority textbook writers.*

REFERENCES

Ahour, T., Towhidiyan, B., & Saeidi, M. (2014). The evaluation of 'English Textbook 2' taught in Iranian high schools from teachers' perspectives. *English Language Teaching, 7*(3), 150–158.

Appadoo-Ramsamy, W. (2022). *Teacher agency: A case study of Mauritius* (Doctoral dissertation).

Bandura, A. (2006). Towards a psychology of human agency. *Perspectives on Psychological Science, 1*(2), 164–180. https://doi.org/10.1111/j.1745-6916.2006.00011.x

Borg, S. (2003). Teacher cognition in language teaching: A review of research on what language teachers think, know, believe, and do. *Language Teaching, 36*(2), 81–109.

Carless, D. (2007). The suitability of task-based approaches for secondary schools: Perspectives from Hong Kong. *System, 35*(4), 595–608.

Carranza, C. P., & Cuayahuiltl, E. R. (2015). Influence of contextual factors on EFL Mexican teachers' beliefs and the use of textbooks. *How, 22*(2), 75–90.

Datnow, A. (2020). The role of teachers in educational reform: A 20-year perspective. *Journal of Educational Change, 21*(3), 431–441.

Ebrahimi, F., & Sahragard, R. (2017). Teachers' perceptions of the new English textbooks in Iranian junior high schools. *Journal of Asia TEFL, 14*(2), 355.

Ghorbani, M. R. (2011). Quantification and graphic representation of EFL textbook evaluation results. *Theory and Practice in Language Studies, 1*(5), 511–520.

Haß, F. (Ed.). (2006). *Fachdidaktik Englisch: Tradition innovation praxis*. Klett.

Hornby, A. S., Wehmeier, S., & Ashby, M. (Eds.). (2000). *Oxford advanced learner's dictionary of current English* (6th ed.). Oxford University Press.

Imants, J., & Van der Wal, M. M. (2020). A model of teacher agency in professional development and school reform. *Journal of curriculum studies, 52*(1), 1–14.

Jawaheer, M. (2019). *Trainee teachers' perceptions towards using constructivist pedagogy to foster deep learning approaches to the study of literature at lower secondary* Edited by: Wafa Zoghbor, Suhair Al Alami, & Thomaï Alexiou, 144.

Jawaheer, M. (2022). Introducing ecopoetry in teacher education to promote sustainable education at lower secondary level in Mauritius. In *Management and leadership for a sustainable Africa, Volume 3: Educating for sustainability outcomes* (pp. 65–85). Springer International Publishing.

Jenkins, G. (2020). Teacher agency: The effects of active and passive responses to curriculum change. *The Australian Educational Researcher, 47*(1), 167–181.

Jinot, B. L. (2017). A critical review of the current education system of Mauritius and the learner discipline problem in Mauritian state secondary schools. *Journal of Education and Social Sciences, 8*(1), 47–55.

Khan, K., Khan, W., Hayat, Y., Ahmad, S. M., & Raza, K. K. (2020). A comparative study of students' and teachers' perceptions about English textbooks at intermediate level and their role in promoting students' proficiency in English. *International Journal of English Linguistics, 10*(2), 40–50.

Korlapu-Bungaree, R. (2020). *English literature teachers' pedagogical choices at upper secondary level: narratives of Mauritian teachers* (Doctoral dissertation).

Kim, J. (2024). Why do teachers not change while the national curriculum repeatedly changes?: The 'Hidden' resistance of teachers in the centralized system of education in South Korea. *International Journal of Educational Development, 109*, 103105.

Kumaravadivelu, B. (2006). *Understanding language teaching: From method to postmethod*. Routledge.

Latif, A., & Mahmoud, M. M. (2012). Teaching a standard-based communicative English textbook series to secondary school students in Egypt: Investigating teachers' practices and beliefs. *English teaching: Practice and critique, 11*(3), 78–97.

Lee, R. N., & Bathmaker, A. M. (2007). The use of English textbooks for teaching English to vocational students in Singapore secondary schools: A survey of teachers' Beliefs. *RELC Journal, 38*(3), 350–374.

Li, S. C., Poon, A. Y., Lai, T. K., & Tam, S. T. (2021). Does middle leadership matter? Evidence from a study of system-wide reform on English language curriculum. *International Journal of Leadership in Education, 24*(2), 226–243.

Mahadeo, S. K. (2006). English language teaching in Mauritius: A need for clarity of vision regarding English language policy. *The International Journal of Language, Society and Culture, 18*, 18–12.

Mauritius Institute of Education. (2016). National Curriculum Framework-Nine Year Continuous Basic Education Grades 7,8 & 9. Reduit, Mauritius.

Mauritius Institute of Education. (2017). Teaching and Learning Syllabus Grades 7, 8 & 9.

Ministry of Education and Human Resources, Tertiary Education and Scientific Research. (2017). *Explaining the NYCBE Reform—The secondary sector*. Ministry of Education and Human Resources, Tertiary Education and Scientific Research.

Mitchell, B., & Buntic, C. G. (2023). Global trends in curriculum reform and development. *Curriculum and Teaching, 38*(1), 27–47.

Nguyen, G. V. (2014). Forms or meaning? Teachers' beliefs and practices regarding task-based language teaching: A Vietnamese case study. *Journal of Asia TEFL, 11*(1), 1–36.

Nunan, D. (1999). *Second language teaching & learning*. Heinle & Heinle Publishers.

Okoth, T. A. (2016). Challenges of implementing a top-down curriculum innovation in English language teaching: Perspectives of form Iii English language teachers in Kenya. *Journal of Education and Practice, 7*(3), 169–177.

Panezai, S. G., & Channa, L. A. (2017). Pakistani government primary school teachers and the English textbooks of Grades 1–5: A mixed methods teachers'-led evaluation. *Cogent Education, 4*(1), 1269712.

Parlindungan, F., Rifai, I., & Safriani, A. (2018). The representation of Indonesian cultural diversity in middle school English textbooks. *Indonesian Journal of Applied Linguistics, 8*(2), 289–302.

Raees, C. (2018). Policies, textbooks, and curriculum constraints to integrating literature into language education: EFL teacher perspectives from Russia. *Pedagogika, 132*(4), 178–196.

Rahimi, M., & Hassani, M. (2012). Attitude towards EFL textbooks as a predictor of attitude towards learning English as a foreign language. *Procedia-Social and Behavioral Sciences, 31*, 66–72.

Rahman, M. M., Johan, M., Selim, S. M. M., Singh, M. K. M., & Shahed, F. H. (2019). Teachers' beliefs and practices of implementing secondary English curriculum reform in Bangladesh: A phenomenological study. *Journal of Asia TEFL, 16*(2), 591.

Rosyida, E. M. R. (2016). Teachers' perceptions toward the use of English textbook. *English Education: Jurnal Tadris Bahasa Inggris, 9*(1), 43–54.

Sahlberg, P. (2021). *Finnish lessons 3.0: What can the world learn from educational change in Finland?* Teachers College Press.

Srakang, L. (2013). *A study of teachers perceptions toward using English textbooks: A case study of 10th grade English teachers in Maha Sarakham Province* (Doctoral dissertation).

Tosun, S. (2013). A comparative study on evaluation of Turkish and English foreign language textbooks. *Procedia-Social and Behavioral Sciences, 70*, 1374–1380.

Tran, N. G., Ha, X. V., & Tran, N. H. (2023). EFL reformed curriculum in Vietnam: An understanding of teachers' cognitions and classroom practices. *RELC Journal, 54*(1), 166–182.

Underwood, P. R. (2012). Teacher beliefs and intentions regarding the instruction of English grammar under national curriculum reforms: A Theory of Planned Behaviour perspective. *Teaching and Teacher Education, 28*(6), 911–925.

Uysal, H. H., & Bardakci, M. (2014). Teacher beliefs and practices of grammar teaching: Focusing on meaning, form, or forms? *South African Journal of Education, 34*(1), 1–16.

Van Steen, M. S. J. (2019). *Attitudes towards learning English as a second language in primary schools in Mauritius* (Master's thesis).

Wallace, C. S., & Priestley, M. (2011). Teacher beliefs and the mediation of curriculum innovation in Scotland: A socio-cultural perspective on professional development and change. *Journal of Curriculum Studies, 43*(3), 357–381.

Wen-Cheng, W., Chien-Hung, L., & Chung-Chieh, L. (2011). Thinking of the textbook in the ESL/EFL Classroom. *English Language Teaching, 4*(2), 91–96.

Yakavets, N., Winter, L., Malone, K., Zhontayeva, Z., & Khamidulina, Z. (2023). Educational reform and teachers' agency in reconstructing pedagogical practices in Kazakhstan. *Journal of Educational Change, 24*(4), 727–757.

Yuasa, K. (2010). English Textbooks in Japan and Korea. *Journal of Pan-Pacific Association of Applied Linguistics, 14*(1), 147–158.

CHAPTER 3

Planning and Implementing the Study

Abstract This chapter outlines the methodological framework of the study, detailing the qualitative approach and case study design employed. It explains the rationale for selecting case studies and the ethical considerations involved in conducting research in real-world classroom settings. The chapter also discusses the data collection methods, including interviews, observations and document analysis, and explains the strategies used to ensure the trustworthiness and credibility of the findings.

Keywords Qualitative approach • Case study • Teacher's practice • Textbook use • Interviews • Non-participant lesson observations • Document analysis • Ethical considerations • Data analysis

3.1 Orientation to the Chapter

In this chapter, we provide a detailed account of the methodological framework we adopted to explore the pedagogical practices of English teachers in Mauritius, more particularly their engagement with the government-endorsed textbooks for Grades 7 to 9. As the following section will explain, we chose a qualitative approach since we sought to capture the complexities of teaching English in diverse school contexts. Our use of case studies provided us with in-depth engagement with the

© The Author(s), under exclusive license to Springer Nature Switzerland AG 2025
Y. D. Mahadeo et al., *Exploring Teachers' Pedagogical Choices in Using Textbooks to Teach English,*
https://doi.org/10.1007/978-3-031-98539-3_3

experiences and beliefs of teachers, thus fostering a more nuanced understanding of how our textbooks were perceived and being used in classrooms.

3.2 Research Design and Approach

Qualitative research design was selected for this study to investigate teachers' pedagogical practices in real-world contexts. We opted for a qualitative research paradigm since it recognises 'the complexity of everyday life, nuances of meaning-making in an every-changing world and the multitude of influences that shape human lived experiences' (DeLyser et al., 2010, p. 6). Qualitative methods enable a deep exploration of participants' lived experiences, beliefs and behaviours (Creswell, 2005), which we felt was appropriate to explore teachers' pedagogical beliefs and practices on the use of the English language textbooks in the classroom. The interpretive nature of this research emphasises understanding participants' perspectives and the meaning they construct around their pedagogical decisions. Interpretivism, as described by Reeves and Hedberg (2002), recognises the complexity of teaching environments and the multitude of factors influencing classroom practice.

This being the first formal investigation on the use of English textbooks produced by the MIE from Grades 7 to 9 in the context of the NYCBE reform, we deemed it more suitable to carry out a detailed and in-depth study of English textbook practices in the local classroom context. One distinctive feature of qualitative research lies in the significance of the actual setting or context as well as the importance of the participants' perspective in generating data (Bogdan & Biklen, 1997). One compelling reason to opt for case studies was that it allowed us to proceed to an in-depth examination of complex phenomena within their real-world context (Yin, 2014). In the case of English educators' textbook usage, this method allowed us to capture the nuanced interactions between teachers, students and the curriculum material in the authentic classroom environment. As Guerrettaz et al. (2021) argue, textbooks are not neutral artefacts but are dynamically recontextualised by teachers and learners in the classroom ecology. We realised that each participant's engagement with the English textbooks in their own classes represented distinct cases to be studied. Case studies are particularly valuable in teacher education research because they provide context-rich insights into the decision-making processes of teachers (Stake, 1995), revealing how broader educational reforms, such as the NYCBE in Mauritius, are interpreted and enacted in practice.

The selection of case studies was guided by the diversity of secondary school types in Mauritius. The inclusion of both private and state schools allowed for comparative insights into how different institutional settings affect textbook use. Each researcher identified one specific participant to observe their lessons in their school context to obtain comprehensive insights into their pedagogical beliefs and practices. Each case study was selected to reflect a variety of school types and teacher experiences and examine the interplay between teachers' beliefs, practices and contextual factors (Borg, 2003). Our aim was to focus on real-life classroom interactions and teacher reflections, to understand the complex realities of textbook usage and to explore the role of teacher agency in using and adapting materials to suit the needs of their learners. We employed a multiple case study design, examining five teachers across four different schools. This approach allowed for both in-depth analysis of individual cases and cross-case comparisons (Stake, 2006). Detailed narratives from each case could thus serve as powerful learning tools for pre-service and in-service educators (Merseth, 1996). In addition, using case studies allowed us to go beyond documenting textbook usage; recent literature suggests the need to not just study the implementation of textbooks but also how it is mediated by teachers and received by students (Garton & Graves, 2014).

We hence explored how teachers exhibited their agency by adapting materials, integrating supplementary resources or using diverse teaching strategies to enhance student learning in their classrooms, thus aligning with recent calls in the field for more qualitative research on teachers' cognitive processes and beliefs regarding instructional materials (Tomlinson & Masuhara, 2018). Besides textbook and curriculum implementation, we were thus able to generate data about the participants' resourcefulness and ability to transform curriculum materials into effective and creative teaching resources, in line with the recent shift towards viewing materials use as a socially situated practice (Guerrettaz et al., 2021), rather than a simple matter of implementation.

Our study documented participants' verbal expressions, actions and perspectives regarding the MIE textbooks, allowing for the generation of rich data that contributed to theory building in the field of textbook use in language teaching. Data analysis followed an inductive approach where emergent patterns and themes were identified from both the research process and participant perspectives (Creswell, 2014). Following appropriate consent procedures, we maintained detailed field notes and recordings to document participant experiences and viewpoints. A research assistant, who was thoroughly briefed on the various research instruments, carried out the transcription and coding of the qualitative data. Each of the researchers documented their findings to ensure accurate representation of participant perspectives. Moreover, the presentation and discussion of findings underwent additional verification by the researchers to maximise the authenticity in capturing our participants' viewpoints. We employed a collaborative methodology which involved regular researcher meetings to discuss the research process, data analysis and peer review of the observation data and interview materials to ensure thematic consistency.

We employed an interpretative approach to examine, explain and comprehend the specific contexts, circumstances and processes informing how participants constructed their textbook-based practices. Using this methodology we emphasised contextual analysis by focusing on the complexity of meaning-making processes (Reeves & Hedberg, 2002; Denzin, 2012) while also facilitating comparisons and deeper reflection on our own researcher observations and our participants' experiences. A grounded theory analytical framework was deemed to be most appropriate for conceptualising the data being generated across the various contexts. Strauss and Corbin (1998, p. 12) conceptualise grounded theory (GT) as "theory that was derived from data, systematically gathered and analysed through the research process". We felt GT to be particularly useful for capturing emergent themes about textbook use and teaching practices in its potential in enabling a rich interpretation of the unique contexts of each school setting. This analytical process was initiated with abstractions generated from preliminary participant interviews, which were subsequently refined through classroom observations, post-classroom interviews (where required) and conducting research interviews (Charmaz & Smith, 2003). We then derived analytic categories directly from the empirical data we had generated.

3.3 Selection of Participants

While we had initially planned to have a fair representation of participants from public and private schools, we eventually decided, from a qualitative standpoint, to opt for a relatively small sample of participants from which we generated rich data to understand English teachers' pedagogical practices. This decision was also motivated by the relative difficulty to find participants willing to engage with the researchers on a research project spanning months, as well as the growing realisation, after a few discussions with potential participants, that not all schools were using the MIE textbook.

Eventually, convenience sampling and snowballing were used to identify potential schools and participants who were using the MIE textbook and willing to be part of the project. Other unforeseen circumstances happened for one researcher who could not carry out observations for her first participant as the latter went on maternity leave. Only one lesson was observed for Participant 5 due to exams and schools' closure during the COVID-19 pandemic. During the research process Participant 2 shifted to a different school in the middle of data production. However, the information generated during the first interview still pertained to the teacher's experiences and her perceptions of the textbook. These were probed into when she shifted to a new teaching context. Finally, the sample resulted in five participants: three from private schools, one from a private confessional school and one from a state school. All of them had at least 2 years of teaching experience and three of them had a qualification related to education and teaching. Table 3.1 summarises some information on the background of the participants.

Table 3.1 Participants' profile

Researcher	Yesha	Rajendra	Kamini	Mangala	Reshma
Participant number/pseudonym	1. Reema	2. Rabiah	3. Rachel	4. Rajesh	5. Vayshi 6. Vedi
School posted and visited	Private non-fee paying	Private non-fee paying	Private non-fee paying	Private/confessional	State
Gender	Female	Female	Female	Male	Female (2)
Years of teaching experience	12 years	Approx 2 years	5 years	Approx 3 years	1. 9 years 2. 10 years
Teaching qualification	BA, PGCE PT	BA, MA	TDS, BA	BA, PGCE and MA	1. BA, MA 2. BA, MSc Educational Technologies

3.4 Generating Data

Multiple data collection methods were employed to ensure a comprehensive understanding of the teachers' practices. The primary data collection tools included semi-structured interviews, non-participant classroom observations and document analysis (transcriptions, field notes and recordings), which were deployed at different stages during the fieldwork.

3.4.1 Interviews

Interviews were the main source of data and were used at different stages in the fieldwork. Semi-structured interviews allowed us more flexibility and ensured more responsiveness from our participants.

Table 3.2 shows the total number of interviews carried out for each of the participants. Except for Participant 4 who had gone on maternity leave and Participant 5 who was affected by school closure, all researchers carried out two interviews—one before classroom observation and a second one at the end of all classroom observations.

Semi-structured interviews allowed us more flexibility and responsiveness. All researchers carried their first interview with the participant before going on the field for classroom observations. All interviews were carried out in person and recorded and transcribed. The first interview (Appendix A: Interview Questions) was meant to get to know the participants and understand their experiences while other prompt questions guided the interview process as per the responses of the participants.

While post-observation interviews were also informally and formally carried out to understand some of the practices of the teachers while they were using the textbook in class. Questions were mostly unstructured as it was dependent on the context and the way the textbook and strategies were used during the classroom observations and the reasons why these choices were made. These were used to triangulate the data emerging

Table 3.2 Number of interviews for each participant

	Participant 1	Participant 2	Participant 3	Participant 4	Participant 4 Participant 5
No. of interviews carried out	5	4	3	2	1 Vayshi 1 Vedi

from classroom observations. Each researcher recorded the conversation or/and wrote down their conversation notes which were sent for transcription to the research assistant. All researchers verified their transcripts to ensure that the data remains close to the participants' perspective. While analysing the interviews and observation transcripts, major themes had started to emerge during the coding process. To have deeper insights and catch further nuances, a last interview session was organised with the participant (Appendix B: Interview Questions).

3.4.2 *Non-participant Lesson Observations*

Non-participant lesson observations were central to understanding how teachers implemented the textbooks in practice. The research team employed field notes and audio recordings to capture the details of classroom interactions, instructional strategies and student responses. An observational checklist was used to ensure consistency in data collection across different schools and teachers.

The use of non-participant observation allowed the researchers to document authentic teaching practices without interfering with the classroom dynamics. This method provided a direct view of how teachers navigated the challenges posed by the textbooks, how they engaged students and how they adapted instructional materials in response to students' needs.

Table 3.3 shows the total number of observations that was carried out.

During the classroom observations, informal interviews allowed for the real-time exploration of teachers' decision-making processes. Post-observation interviews were crucial in reflecting on specific pedagogical choices, allowing teachers to articulate their rationale for adapting or supplementing the textbooks. These interviews provided rich data on the challenges teachers faced, the resources they used and their perceptions of the textbook's alignment with students' needs.

Table 3.3 Total number of observations

	Participant 1	Participant 2	Participant 3	Participant 4	Participant 6
No. of observations carried out	3	3	5	4	1

In addition to those main data production instruments, we also analysed relevant documents including the English textbooks being used, the teachers' lesson plans (where available) and any supplementary materials used in observed lessons. This analysis provided context for us to understand the teachers' pedagogical choices and adaptations of textbook content.

3.4.3 Ethical Considerations

Ethical considerations were paramount in this study, particularly given the sensitivity of classroom observations and interviews with practising teachers. This study adhered to strict ethical guidelines to protect the anonymity and confidentiality of the participants and schools involved in the study and pseudonyms were used to anonymise their identities. To obtain ethical clearance from gatekeepers, we negotiated access to the different schools through potential participants. Rectors were informed about the project, and their permission was sought to observe the participants in class. We obtained informed consent from all participants, clearly explaining the study's purpose, procedures and potential risks/benefits. Participants were informed of their right to withdraw from the study at any time, and their permission was always sought prior to audio recording interviews. All personal data, transcriptions and recordings were securely stored on a password-protected database, accessible only to the research team. Any potentially identifying information was removed or modified in research reports, without compromising the integrity of the information we produced. This measure ensured that our participants could speak freely about their experiences without fear of repercussion. The study also considered the sensitive nature of classroom observations, ensuring that no undue pressure was placed on the teachers during data collection. We were mindful of maintaining a non-intrusive presence in the classrooms and respected the participants' professional boundaries throughout the study.

In carrying out this study, we were very sensitive to our positionality: as teacher educators and curriculum writers, we were conscious that researching how educators use textbooks we had authored would present potential risks and ethical concerns that needed careful consideration and mitigation.

Firstly, we endeavoured to ensure that, in terms of researcher positionality, there was limited potential for bias both in data collection and in interpretation (Ravitch & Carl, 2021). We were mindful that, as curriculum writers ourselves, our close connection to the research phenomenon could inadvertently affect our objectivity. One instance could be for us to, consciously or unconsciously, seek out or highlight data that would confirm our expectations as to how the textbook should be used. We thus had to address this risk of confirmation bias through our prior discussions as well as debriefings after meeting the participants. We also scrutinised our transcripts to check whether we were leading a particular position on textbook usage, or whether we were unduly influencing the participants.

We were also mindful of the impact of indirectly initiating a power dynamic through what could be construed as a vertical relationship. What if the participants felt pressured to report positive experiences or align their practices with the researchers' expectations, during the class observations, out of fear of professional consequences? Such a power imbalance could lead to skewed data and impact upon the validity of our research findings (Tisdell, 2017).

To mediate these risks and ensure ethical soundness (Hammersley and Traianou, 2012), we proceeded as follows:

- To ensure transparency and reflexivity, and mitigate unconscious biases (Finlay, 2002), we explicitly acknowledged our position and potential biases in the research design, data production and reporting stages.
- We clearly communicated our roles as researchers and clarified expectations on both sides when initiating contact with the participants. This was even more important due to the different roles we played as curriculum writers, teacher educators and researchers. This allowed us to reassure our participants that their honest feedback would be valued and would not have negative consequences.
- We implemented robust measures to protect participants' identities and ensure confidentiality to alleviate concerns about professional repercussions and encourage honest responses (Kaiser, 2009). In a small island context like ours, schools and participants could easily be recognised through one casual description or reference, and participants were keen to remain anonymous, which we ensured at our end.
- We ensured, where possible, to allow participants to review and comment on the data produced and its interpretation to ensure that their perspectives were accurately represented. (Birt et al., 2016)

3.5 Data Analysis

The analysis followed a grounded theory approach (Strauss & Corbin, 1998), in which data were systematically coded and categorised to identify emergent themes inductively identified from the data. All interviews and classroom observations were transcribed verbatim by a research assistant who was thoroughly briefed on the study's context and objectives. Researchers then reviewed the transcripts for accuracy and to begin familiarising themselves with the data. Open coding was initially used to break down the data into discrete parts, with each segment of the interview and observation transcripts being analysed for significant patterns. Initially, each of us independently coded our own data sets, identifying key concepts and potential themes. Axial coding was then used to link these patterns to broader categories that aligned with the study's research questions, such as teacher perceptions, pedagogical choices and challenges in textbook implementation.

Throughout the data analysis process, our research team employed a collaborative peer-checking method to ensure the reliability of the findings. A collaborative approach to data analysis ensured that the team, while perhaps holding different viewpoints on the design and implementation of textbooks, still agreed to discuss matters and ensure that we maintained rigour not only in the generation of data but also in the discussion of findings. Regular meetings were held to review coding decisions, discuss emerging themes and ensure that the data analysis remained grounded in the participants' perspectives. This collaborative approach also contributed to the refinement of thematic categories and relationships, ensuring that the final analysis accurately reflected the complexities of the teachers' experiences. Once our individual case analyses were complete, we carried out a cross-case analysis to identify patterns, similarities and differences across the different cases. This process allowed us to develop more robust findings that could account for the diversity of school and classroom contexts we encountered in the field. Throughout the research process, we also engaged in ongoing reflexivity through team discussions, and individual reflections, which we shared at different points in the research process and helped us to critically examine our assumptions and biases. This approach strengthened the reliability of the findings and the credibility of the analysis and ensured that multiple perspectives were considered in the final write-up.

3.6 Ensuring Trustworthiness and Credibility

We employed several strategies to ensure the trustworthiness and credibility of our findings. We ensured that the data was rich and deep through saturation by engaging with multiple sources and instruments such as interviews, observations and documents, as well as multiple researchers to corroborate findings and arrive at a more comprehensive understanding of the phenomenon under study. Our methodological approach involved a collaborative analysis approach, that is, iterative, team-based data analysis sessions leading to peer debriefing, collaborative coding, methodological decisions and discussions on emerging findings and potential biases. This approach towards collective inquiry in educational research ensured that we ironed out the possibilities for bias and error to seep into the data and the analysis. Throughout the research process, we engaged in ongoing reflexivity through team discussions and individual journaling. This practice helped us critically examine our own assumptions and biases, enhancing the trustworthiness of our findings. Member checking was also used, depending on the availability of the participants, where we shared preliminary findings with them, inviting them to provide feedback and clarification. This process helped to ensure that our interpretations accurately represented their perspectives and experiences.

3.7 Limitations

For qualitative studies such as this one, one major challenge was in finding participants willing to invest the time and energy required to engage with the study. It was also challenging to find participants from different typologies of schools. With this in mind, it was understood that the views of the participants about their own textbook practices could not be generalised since they were context- and participant-specific. We prioritised having deep authentic understanding of textbook usage in specific classroom settings and thus do not claim to have a comparative understanding and deeper insights about textbook practices in private and state schools. The depth of data collected through case studies provided rich, context-specific insights that are valuable for understanding the nuanced ways in which teachers engage with English textbooks in the Mauritian context.

Finally, our engagement with each case was hampered by the COVID-19 pandemic and ensuing nationwide school closure, which impacted on the duration of the study, extending it for one more year. As a result, the number of classroom observations was reduced, and some participants were unavailable for follow-up interviews. Despite these challenges, the data collected were sufficient to address the research questions and provide meaningful insights into the use of the government-endorsed textbooks in Mauritius.

3.8 Conclusion

Using a qualitative, multiple case study approach in this study enabled us to explore teachers' pedagogical practices and decision-making processes in using English language textbooks in a more nuanced way. Our combination of in-depth interviews, classroom observations and document analysis across different school contexts enabled us to generate rich data that shed light upon the complex situation of textbook implementation in the Mauritian secondary school system. While the study was itself limited in terms of scope and sample size, this approach nevertheless provided valuable insights which we feel would be relevant to both researchers and practitioners in the field of English language teaching.

References

Birt, L., Scott, S., Cavers, D., Campbell, C., & Walter, F. (2016). Member checking: A tool to enhance trustworthiness or merely a nod to validation? *Qualitative Health Research*, *26*(13), 1802–1811. https://doi.org/10.1177/1049732316654870

Bogdan, R. C., & Biklen, S. K. (1997). Qualitative research for education: An introduction to theory and methods. Allyn & Bacon.

Borg, S. (2003). Teacher cognition in language teaching: A review of research on what language teachers think, know, believe, and do. *Language Teaching*, *36*(2), 81–109.

Charmaz, K., & Smith, J. A. (2003). Grounded theory. In J. A. Smith (Ed.), *Qualitative psychology: A practical guide to research methods* (pp. 81–110). SAGE Publications.

Creswell, J. W. (2005). *Educational research: Planning, conducting, and evaluating quantitative and qualitative research* (2nd ed.). Pearson Education.

Creswell, J. W. (2014). *Research design: Qualitative, quantitative, and mixed methods approaches* (4th ed.). SAGE Publications.

DeLyser, D., Herbert, S., Aitken, S., Crang, M., & McDowell, L. (2010). *The SAGE handbook of qualitative geography*. SAGE Publications.

Denzin, N. K. (2012). *The research act: A theoretical introduction to sociological methods* (3rd ed.). Aldine Transaction.

Finlay, L. (2002). 'Outing' the researcher: The provenance, process, and practice of reflexivity. *Qualitative Health Research, 12*(4), 531–545. https://doi.org/10.1177/104973202129120052

Garton, S., & Graves, K. (2014). Identifying a research agenda for language teaching materials. *Modern Language Journal, 98*(2), 654–657.

Guerrettaz, A. M., Engman, M. M., & Matsumoto, Y. (2021). Empirically defining language learning and teaching materials in use through sociomaterial perspectives. *Modern Language Journal, 105*(S1), 3–20. https://doi.org/10.1111/modl.12691.

Hammersley, M., & Traianou, A. (2012). *Ethics in qualitative research: Controversies and contexts.* SAGE Publications.

Kaiser, K. (2009). Protecting respondent confidentiality in qualitative research. *Qualitative Health Research, 19*(11), 1632–1641. https://doi.org/10.1177/1049732309350879.

Merseth, K. K. (1996). Cases and case methods in teacher education. In J. Sikula (Ed.), *Handbook of research on teacher education* (2nd ed., pp. 722–744). Macmillan.

Ravitch, S. M., & Carl, N. M. (2021). *Qualitative research: Bridging the conceptual, theoretical, and methodological* (2nd ed.). SAGE Publications.

Reeves, T. C., & Hedberg, J. G. (2002). *Interactive learning systems evaluation.* Educational Technology Publications.

Stake, R. E. (1995). *The art of case study research.* SAGE Publications.

Stake, R. E. (2006). *Multiple case study analysis.* The Guilford Press.

Strauss, A., & Corbin, J. (1998). *Basics of qualitative research: Techniques and procedures for developing grounded theory* (2nd ed.). SAGE Publications.

Tisdell, E. J. (2017). Adult education and lifelong learning. In L. R. S. Steinberg (Ed.), *Contemporary theories of learning: Learning theorists ... in their own words* (2nd ed., pp. 234–243). Routledge.

Yin, R. K. (2014). *Case study research: Design and methods* (5th ed.). SAGE Publications.

CHAPTER 4

The Voices of the Drivers of Curricular Reform

Abstract This chapter presents the findings of the research conducted in Mauritius, offering insights into the diverse ways teachers perceive and use the government-endorsed English textbooks, conceptualised, designed and written by minority textbook writers, employed by Mauritius Institute of Education (MIE). Through vignettes, the chapter explores the pedagogical choices teachers make, the challenges they face and the ways they adapt these textbooks to suit their students' needs. The chapter highlights the importance of teacher agency and adaptability in maximising the effectiveness of textbooks.

Keywords Case study • Textbook use • Pedagogical choices • Teacher agency • Teacher perceptions and beliefs • Challenges in use of textbooks • Resources

4.1 Orientation to the Chapter

This chapter is a representation of the data that was produced with our four participants. This chapter is mounted as four case studies. Each case study is made up of a basic portrait of our individual participant, their perceptions on the textbook and their pedagogical choices that informed the use of the textbooks we conceptualised, designed and wrote. As mentioned in the methodology chapter, the data has been constructed from a mix of interviews as well as observation of the classes of our participants. This chapter only puts forth a first-level analysis, which will be developed fully in the two chapters that follow.

4.2 REEMA: THE ACE DRIVER

This case study explores Reema's perceptions of the government-endorsed textbook as well as the pedagogical choices she makes when using the government-endorsed textbook in her English language classroom. The study is based on an analysis of interview data and classroom observations, highlighting the teacher's strategies, content coverage and use of various resources.

Reema is in her late thirties and has approximately thirteen years of teaching experience. She has graduated with her Postgraduate Certificate in Education at the MIE a few years ago. When I started fieldwork with her, I quickly realised that she had her own brand of teaching. She had strong teacher agency, and her teaching style was fed by her personality and the way she conceptualised and understood teaching and learning. She uses the textbook, although her head of department has discouraged its usage, but she uses other materials, and she makes use of resources that she prepares also. She very often repeats that "at times, people don't know what I am doing in my class" because she does not stick to the traditional way of teaching the textbooks or teaching to exams. However, Reema's class is very warm, and she has a strong rapport with all the students with whom she works. She calls them "my kids". She has her own brand of classroom discipline, and her students listen to her because she has built a good rapport with them. The students, who look up to Reema, respect and like her a lot and listen to her instructions and work according to her teaching style. She normally takes quite some time in helping them develop essential strategies that they will use in her class, as is evidenced by the following lines.

R: To teach everything … yeah? You tally all the skills just trying to understand, you use the questions given in the reading comprehension; the two types of question. You use all of them?
T: … because as I said, uh, yeah most of them, because as I said, I don't know what type of exams they're gonna have. So, the more uncomfortable I make them, the more sure I am that they can tackled the questions properly.

Hence, if she gives the students independent work using her Google classrooms, they make the effort to go through the materials that she shares before coming to her class. When she teaches, she encourages all children to participate and allows them to tell her what they want, creating the right space for them to engage with her. For those who have problems, she encourages and motivates them so that they can cope with any learning challenges they face. In many ways, Reema is the central figure in the children's lives in the world of the classroom and her pedagogical choices are dictated by their learning needs, so she uses the ping pong mode of teaching to be able to meet her learners' needs.

4.2.1 Perceptions of the Textbooks

Although the government-endorsed textbooks have been prescribed by the Ministry of Education as textbooks, our participants have varied perceptions about them. Reema, who has been advised by her head of the department not to use the textbook in her classes, bypasses the authority of her head and chooses to make use of the textbooks at the various levels she is teaching. The participants of this study also highlight the inadequacy of the textbooks when it comes to the level of the students that they teach. Reema, who is based in an urban private-aided school and who confirms that she likes the textbook, claims that "the level is high. Because, like, today when we did the theatre one, the kids didn't understand the passage at all". She, further, adds that "there are some things that are a bit too difficult for the kids".

On the other hand, Reema believes that the textbook is important as it develops the different competencies that are a prerequisite for the national exams and she states that she wants "them to have a feel of the different types of passages because we have no clue as teachers, what's coming for the exams". **She, therefore, feels that the MIE textbooks are going to influence the setting of the national exams and claims that "[t]he reason being that the exams are going to be similar, if not, exactly the same as MIE".**

Reema, thus, adapts the different activities proposed by the textbook to suit her teaching purpose. Hence, she clearly states that she does not use the books "completely" as she does not "compartmentalise". She has a multipronged approach to using a comprehension text. She, therefore, amalgamates the usage of the textbook to suit her teaching style and also meet her objectives set out for her teaching, whether it is teaching of grammar, oral skills, reading or writing skills. Reema feels that the textbook does not really cater to her students' needs directly and that this, thus, entails more effort on her part to ensure that her students understand the content of the textbook. She keeps on repeating in her interviews that she likes the textbooks, stating that she "like(s) the variety and diversity. I also like the way the comprehension passages have been, you know, it's not like just the stories then answer questions. I like the format of the different passages".

Moreover, Reema adapts her teaching to ensure that she teaches her students numerous skills so that they can be prepared to sit for exams, as she believes that her students are not "high flyers". Speaking about their level, she mentions the challenges she faces when teaching them and this has an influence on the different choices that she makes:

T: Because my kids are not very, uh,—not very smart or they—very lazy, I don't know. Many times, I threatened them; "let's go for a walk near the river, I'll drown you and say 'Bubye' to you" and "lazy, lazy. My god! Lazy!" So, they do. ... Also, they don't have the appropriate vocabulary. The passages are pretty difficult for them.

She, therefore, makes certain pedagogical choices that will cater to her teaching purpose, which is equipping her students with the different skills that will be necessary to sit for the exams, as is evidenced in the extract below:

T: Directly, no. ... But that's why I taught them the template and I taught them reverse comprehension. Cause the point is; when passages are difficult, I make them realise that the questions are easier and then they can make sense of them, through the questions.
R: Okay, so you beef up with strategies and techniques, basically, to teach reading leisure, but each text comes with a pre reading, and that is not enough for your kids?
T: Uh, it depends when I have time, because ... and if it tallies with the way I'm working ... because it might not tally with the way I'm working and uh, the common point is to make the kids use their brains ... cause if I go according to the book, they really try and don't use the brain and they don't even try to you know, you take a try and throw him in water; he gonna keep sinking instead of trying to survive. So that's what I do to them and I try to show them the connection between all 4 skills through the ....

She speaks of the necessity of having to craft her teaching to ensure that they use their brains and she does so by devising different strategies and techniques and coming up with additional resources as has been highlighted previously. This is illustrated in the extract below, where she puts forth her own position regarding the choices that she makes:

R: To teach everything … yeah? You tally all the skills just trying to understand, you use the questions given in the reading comprehension; the two types of question. You use all of them?
T: … because as I said, uh, yeah most of them, because as I said, I don't know what type of exams they're gonna have. So, the more uncomfortable I make them, the surer I am that they can tackled the questions properly.
R: So, you try and make them uncomfortable.
T: Not uncomfortable but …
Take them out of their comfort zone …
Because otherwise, their brains are asleep. You've seen that. Anyone in class, you've seen that ….

4.2.2 Reema's Pedagogical Choices in Using Government-Endorsed Textbooks

It was noted that most teachers accompany the teaching of the textbook with a range of pedagogical strategies. As discussed in the earlier section, such is the case of Reema also. The main strategy used by Reema whilst using the materials is mostly questioning. She uses questioning to get the students to interact for different purposes. Hence, she uses questioning, not only to further discussion when she is teaching but also to drive in major concepts around the teaching of writing and develop the writing competencies of the students, as can be seen in the extracts below.

T: I don't. Because sometimes it is a little difficult for me to find a story … so it's easier to think of setting for example. Remember last time we did the dessert, if you have the dessert and you have the ocean, so it is resistant?
S: no

T: Cinderella ... space, the story says this here? Sometimes you have to find which one is easier for you, right? What are the elements, what are the narrative elements you are going to use in this particular story?
T: climax ... atan ... what is your start? We always have a start, and we always have a finish. Correct, what is your start? Look at your first picture. When? What is he doing?
T: alors the climax will be when she meets the grandmother ... climax bizin involve the main character. Right? So what is the most important story in that story? Sorry, what is the most important event in that story?
[S reply]

Moreover, independent research work, though not always feasible, is also encouraged by Reema. Apart from teaching different language skills, Reema also focuses on developing different competencies as well as attitudes, namely the ability for independent study. She provides students with video materials and allows Internet searches so that they can develop the ability to carry out their work alone.

R: so you have asked them to read silently and understand ....
T: [...] it's useless to make them read sentence per sentence and it is wastage of time and this type of reading should be read in mind off asleep, the rest of them would be asleep. And it's completely to me, pointless because for the exams I won't be there. So what I do is the purpose of sending the videos to them, somehow will catch their attention. So either for the whole passage,
R: but you've already provided the ground for understanding or what about the tough words basically?
T: they got google for ...
R: okay so they look up the word on google, so you allow them to use mobile phone as a tool in a classroom.

At times, she complements independent study with pair work so that they can discuss and clarify any misconception. She also gets them to correct their own work so that they develop the skill of editing their work.

S: we can work with our pairs?
T: you are supposed to work with your pairs ... if you have any problem, you call me.
[S get to work with pairs while discussing with each other]

Reema also makes use of additional resources to teach in her classroom. It was noted that Reema, who works in an urban private-aided school, uses the activities and texts provided in the MIE Grades 7 to 9 flexibly and adapts them to her teaching purpose. She shows her agency by making use of the different activities as well as texts provided to teach for different purposes. Given that she teaches the skills in an integrated manner and that she doesn't 'compartmentalize', she can take a text and use it for a quick test to "give" her students "an appeal of working a comprehension in 10 minutes". This is to get them to develop the skills of answering questions in limited time.

She also uses some of the texts to teach the concept of plot, character, setting and themes which would then serve to consolidate students' writing skills. She also uses reading texts to teach grammar. She also embeds within her teaching the teaching of literature. She, therefore, can use one text for multiple purposes depending on what her teaching objective and target is. She uses mostly the reading texts provided by the textbook and does not use the textbook as much for writing activities. Concerning the teaching of the oral part, she uses the resources that were provided with the textbooks and downloaded them online for usage in class. This is evidenced by the extract below.

R: I'm trying to understand. Uh, forget: 'how often you use the textbook'. Can we just come to how you use it? Like, say, in your week, you've just given me an example of reading. Let's take it grade wise. So, Grade 8, what do you use it for? You told me …

T: Passages, both of them.

R: Only for reading comprehension?

T: As, I told you I'm doing comprehension right now. I'll do a number of passages, one after the other, because I am tallying it with essay writing. So, because I have taught the kids. … I am trying to drill it into their heads; plot character, setting, themes and so on. I started with narrative composition. I am shifting now to comprehension; using the theme techniques and then, I'll shift them to literature. So, while I'm doing, uh, essays comprehension, I am also doing certain grammar parts.

Res: So, you're teaching it as a whole. I can get that.

T: But I did use it for oral.

Res: You use it for your oral?

T: For oral classes, because I have my own speaker and my own projector. So, uh, I downloaded the audios from the website and I played it in class a few times as we did for … so ….

R: You're teaching them listening then? And speaking as well? Do you use the textbook then; when you are teaching them listening and speaking? You told me, you use for comprehension uh let's take … is it the same for Grade 8 and 9? You … okay? You said, you teach them a number of passages. Give me some examples of how you take it across, because one unit comprises of 2 text? Reading, writing, vocabulary, reading for appreciation, do you use the textbook to teach all of these reading aspects?

Reema makes use of an extensive array of materials to complement the usage of the textbook. Whilst she uses the texts offered for different purposes, she supplements her teaching using PowerPoint presentations which she has prepared in advance.

T: Like today, I did for Form 2, grade 8, I did unit 4. So, the first 2 passages; theatre and the one that was after, Which also had to do with theatre. So now, what I have to do, since I have tomorrow and I'm not working with grade 8, I will have time to go and prepare, uh, check the passage; see what they are talking about, and then prepare a sort of 'PowerPoint' with videos and …

She has also integrated within her practice the usage of Google classrooms, with which she already familiarised her students, and she also supplements her teaching and usage of the MIE Grades 7 to 9 textbooks through online resources that she finds and uses to suit her teaching purpose. This can be observed in the extracts below:

T: this is the template I used for every single story. So, it falls under story telling. This is Google classroom, it falls under story telling. This is a template I referred them. So, it's regardless of whether it is euh, comprehension, literature.

T: obviously I took inspiration from the internet.

R: very nice. You know why I'm saying that because I've seen that in a teaching practice class, that's why I'm asking where from, I thought it was from literature class.

T: that's it. That's why it on the story telling.

R: so this is from literature right?
T: it's for everything, I use it for comprehension, I use it for literature and I use it for essay writing, because the concept is the same, so the point is to make them understand, that's it. As long as it's a story, it's exactly the same ....
R: and you've mentioned google classroom so you have a google classroom for them.
T: yeah I have a google classroom for them
R: so you give them tasks to do,
T: yeah, this is my friend ... 8th literature
R: what do you do? You put up tasks ....
T: you will see, no one likes online classes so I've got two on Saturdays or Sundays and ...
R: so that's extra that you are doing, on top and above of your classes.
T: but many times I sent them a homework or notes.

4.2.3 Analysis

It was noted that Reema's pedagogical choices were embedded in her personal beliefs, knowledge as well as the experience she had of teaching and her own personal teaching style. It is to be added that although Reema followed the PGCE course, she attributes her choices to her own beliefs and styles, stating that the course only confirmed her personal beliefs and style.

Reema's knowledge and understanding of her students takes centre stage in her teaching and the choices she makes when using the textbook. She constantly thrusts the concept of the level of her students forward, justifying the choices that she makes, whether it is using the textbook as well as any other strategies or resources that she adds to the teaching and learning process. Not only does she have a very good rapport with her students, but she plans and organises her work around what she feels would be better for them, what would allow them to develop the requisite competencies, skills and attitudes and what would allow them to sit for the exams with success. Her teaching is, therefore, very student-centred and delineates from the traditional approaches to teaching.

The need to ensure that her students, who she feels do not have a good level, develop the requisite skills and competencies to sit for exams and pass them determines the different choices of strategies as well as resources that she opts for. Although her school does not encourage the choice of the government-endorsed textbooks, she chooses to override her head of department's choices and opinions because she believes that the textbook has valuable resources that allow her to amalgamate her teaching with the use of other resources and strategies. In so doing, she shows strong teacher agency by letting her teaching and learning beliefs override her choices. Hence, she believes that the way the texts have been conceptualised and designed prepare learners to develop the necessary competencies and skills that would be valuable to pass the exams with success. However, she does not stick to being textbook-oriented and amalgamates her teaching with an additional choice of strategies as resources which form the crux of her teaching. Adaptability and flexibility are key concepts that drive her pedagogical choices.

One of the ways that she chooses to do so is using Google classrooms, which she prepares and gives access to her students, thereby encouraging them to work independently on their own. Very often, she sends them materials and resources which they need to read and work on before coming to class and when they come to class, she encourages them to use the space to bring up their own opinions or questions they might have. She does not limit herself to working within the teaching hours but stretches learning beyond working hours, therefore using her classes only to maximise on the learning process. She focuses on teaching the four language skills and ensures that she makes space for oral and aural skills in class as well, teaching also listening skills. She also embeds within her teaching, the teaching of grammar as well as vocabulary. She uses the integrated approach to teach and is flexible enough to adapt the different reading texts designed in the textbook to her teaching purpose. Hence, she can use a listening text to teach reading and use a reading text to teach grammar. Thus, Reema's pedagogical choices are not only student-centred but focus on learning as key experience but is also determined by her own teacher style and her knowhow at integrating material design as well as technology and use of diverse strategies in her class. In working in such a flexible manner, Reema privileges the development of the different language skills and competencies which she feels are important for the exams. **She, further, embodies the philosophy that governs the NYCBE reform and is a conscious and active driver of the reform in her own practice. These are governed by her own teacher agency more than the document and the philosophy it expounds.**

4.2.4 Noted Challenges and Limitations

Although Reema likes the textbook conceptualised and designed by MIE, she also feels that the textbook is not always appropriate for her students who cannot access the texts as 'highflyers' would access them. She feels that the textbook is not level appropriate for her students, and this, therefore, leads to her having to choose other materials and resources to supplement her teaching. She feels that some of the questions set out for the reading comprehensions are of 'high level' for her students. Moreover, although it does not pose an issue to her, Reema feels that **the paucity of grammar exercises is one of the reasons that most teachers do not prefer the government-endorsed textbooks.** She points out that she feels that the MIE textbooks are ideal to prepare students to sit for exams, but she feels that given that the textbook has been designed as per the philosophy underpinning the NYCBE reform and is learner-centered as well as activity-based, most teachers feel that the books do not drive students towards the exams. Personally, the only issue Reema has with the textbook is its level.

4.3 Vedi: The Obedient Driver

Vedi is 37 years old and has 13 years of teaching experience in state secondary schools. She has three areas of expertise namely; English, educational technology and performing arts & music. She holds a BA (Hons) in English and MA in Educational Technology from the University of Mauritius. She also holds a BA in Performing Arts and Diploma in Vocal Hindustani and Violin.

4.3.1 Perceptions of Textbooks

Although Vedi perceives the textbook as being resourceful, she allows her students, especially the 'highflyers', to be creative and not limit themselves to examples provided in the textbook. However, she admits that the 'low achievers', who have difficulty with creative writing, would benefit from examples provided in the textbook. She believes that what suits her teaching is an adaptation of the exercises in the textbook.

R: So, you usually use the textbook.
T: I use the textbook. But I do adapt certain exercises in my own way of teaching.

4.3.2 Vedi's Pedagogical Choices in Using Government-Endorsed Textbooks

It was noted that Vedi made her own choices when it came to the use of the textbooks and the activities within the textbooks. She affirmed that she would recommend the MIE textbooks because they contain a wide range of interesting activities which leads to the teaching of the different skills. She, also, added that the activities are varied in the different chapters of the book, hence providing exposure to students to many ways of learning the English language. However, in the state secondary school where Vedi is currently posted, she believes that her students are "high flyers" and she feels that some activities might be limited for them; she adapts her teaching to suit their level as illustrated below:

R: Okay. How do you generally use the textbook? When I observed your lessons, I saw that you were using the same activities in the textbook and I remember you told me that you were not using the example that was given in the textbook but you were advising your students to come up with their own examples. I remember there was a writing activity where the beginning was already provided but you told them they could write their own introduction.

T: Well, it's true that I don't do all the activities in the same way that is given for e.g., if there are examples given for example for the activity we were working on. I think it was writing a postcard. There was an introduction that was already provided but I found that if you limit students to using those examples, everybody will be using the same thing. So, I wanted them to come up with some creativity in their writing. And that's why I advise them to devise their own way of writing the introduction. That's also because before that lesson, I had already explained how to write an introduction creatively. So, I used that activity to actually enhance what I have already taught in class. So that's why I did not really limit myself to whatever was given in the textbook. And I think that this is a good idea. … The textbook is there to help us, true. For example, to assist students. … Because we have different types of learners. For example, in my class, we have mixed abilities. So, maybe for a lower. … A low achiever might have certain difficulty coming up with a creative piece of writing. So that example might be helpful to them. But for all those high flyers. … All those students who can strive to do better. So, I think. It's good to adapt whatever has been provided according to the needs of the students.

Vedi, further, explained how she adapted the activities in the textbook. She believes that whatever is provided in the textbook can be used as a guide to start the lesson. She mentioned that adaptations depend on the class size. According to her, some activities cannot be conducted unless the class (e.g., with 43 students) is split into groups or pairs. In other words, she adapted her lessons and strategies to cater to different types and needs of her students.

R   Do you adapt the text according to the ability of you learners or to produce specific knowledge? How would you say you usually adapt the textbook?

T: I adapt to suit the specific needs and also abilities of students. But also, depending on whatever aims I have set for that lesson, what I want them to achieve at the end of that lesson. So, depending on that, I do adapt the lessons.

R: Would you like to give me some examples of how you've adapted, may be to produce a specific knowledge or maybe according to the ability of your learners?

T: For example, in literature class, I do adapt very often. So, for example, for the poem, 'chimney sweeper', there were specific questions that were given … in the text. But, then, I made them do other activities besides what was given in the text. Because I had a huge number of students and also because I wanted them to think about the text in a different way. Not only limiting themselves to only seeing the poem as a story that they have to learn or the poetic devices used in it. e.g. This is a simile. This is an alliteration etc. … So, I just wanted them to feel actually what was going on in the poem and try to relate it to whatever they know nowadays. So, for e.g., comparing how people long ago were living. What were the problems that they were facing with child labor? And what they know about child labor today … Issues still being recurrent. … In that way, I did some activities where, for e.g., I made them do class presentation or project work where they could come up with some research on their own and understand properly how this problem of child labor could affect them.

Vedi provides examples of how she adapted the activities in the textbook for the literature component and how she implemented them. For instance, she tries to relate the topic to the prior knowledge of learners;

she encourages some research work on the theme of the poem and planned class presentation and project work. She gets learners to develop their own views on the topic of the poem.

In her teaching of English grammar, Vedi affirms that she has to adapt every time since there are not many grammar exercises in the textbook.

T: For the grammar section, I do adapt every time … because I personally think that the amount of grammar exercises that have been given in the textbook is quite less compared to what I think the students should be given. So, most of the time when I do specific chapters, for example, I'm explaining about active/passive, I use the explanation in the text to start with. … We discuss about it. We take the examples etc. But then I have to support with other materials, and I have to give them additional work in order to achieve whatever standard I have set for that lesson.

Vedi usually prepares additional materials and activities other than what are provided in the textbooks. However, she admits that she never prepared any reading materials for reading comprehension classes. She uses the texts/passages provided in the textbook.

Moreover, Vedi, who uses the textbook in her teaching, also makes use of questioning as a strategy to drive the brainstorming to generate ideas for the writing task that the students are supposed to carry out.

As far as teaching the oral component is concerned, Vedi confirms that she teaches the "oral" component lesser "(b)ecause (she) find(s) it comes along with the reading comprehension itself, it is already there, so they are already reading". In this way, she maximises the use of the passages/texts provided in the textbook to teach the oral component, side by side. In other words, she does not implement the activities provided in the textbook for the development of oral skills but rather integrates the teaching of oral skills in her reading comprehension classes, where she initiates discussions for the learners to contribute orally.

4.3.3 *Analysis*

Vedi demonstrated the ability to be creative when it came to making her own choices while using the textbooks and the activities in them. For instance, she modifies activities provided in the textbooks to suit the profile of her learners. It was noted that the teachers get creative when they handle the government endorsed textbook, therefore making them collaborative contributors of the textbook. Vedi, usually, creates her own materials and activities rather than relying only on the ones suggested or provided in the textbook. As such, she complements the materials and activities with those that she has created herself. This choice enables her to, in turn, develop the creativity of learners. Baleghizadeh and Dargahi (2016) assert that such moves on the part of the teacher can develop creativity in learners. While moving beyond the textbook, Vedi demonstrates that she understands the importance of improving instruction and enhancing learning through complementary materials and activities.

According to Vedi, the materials and activities provided in the textbooks are inadequate. Vedi recognises the constraints of the textbooks. For instance, she mentioned that she has to adapt activities for grammar all the time. Tomlinson (2015) asserts the importance of challenging teachers to use textbooks creatively. The books that we conceptualised, designed and wrote have, therefore, led to this. It has led teachers to move beyond the resource they have in hand, adapt it and use it to suit their purpose, rather than adhering to it as they would adhere to biblical scriptures. Moving beyond our positions as minority textbook writers, one of our aims as academics who also train teachers has always been to empower them to use any resource at hand with such creativity. We have noted that Vedi shows the ability to adapt the textbook and its activities as an **experienced** teacher. Although she has not been trained by the MIE, she is acting as per her own teacher cognition and agency.

Hence, we have noted that Vedi does not implement the oral activities set in the textbooks. She rather integrates the oral skills when teaching reading comprehension. This choice is guided by the fact that she **believes** that it is more important to concentrate on reading comprehension rather than oral activities since **oral skills are not assessed in lower secondary.** This suggests that teachers use the textbooks to teach what they consider as being the most important skills but decide to integrate oral skills while discussing comprehension passages. However, the oral activities in the textbooks consist of instructions, strategies and questions which are pertinent to develop oral skills in a more spontaneous manner. Although developing oral skills through discussion on a text is commendable, textbook writers need to reflect on whether the oral activities are too ambitious for the teachers who need to implement them, when they are governed by an exam system which gives near to zero importance to the teaching and assessing of oral skills.

4.4 Pranav: The Entitled Driver

Based on the analysis of interview data and classroom observations, this case study explores Pranav's perceptions of the government-endorsed textbooks. It further uncovers his pedagogical choices (including teaching strategies, content coverage and use of alternative textbooks and resources) when teaching English.

Pranav is in his mid-thirties, with seven years of teaching experience. He worked as a supply teacher for the first two years before being appointed on a full-time basis as a permanent teacher in the same school. Incidentally, it is the same school where he was an alumnus. Pranav has specialised in English. After his BA (Hons) in English, he completed his PGCE and then read for an MA in English. Pranav enjoys teaching but aspires to move up the professional ladder and wants to specialise in school leadership and management in the future to better prepare for managerial positions.

4.4.1 Perceptions of the Textbook

Data analysis indicates that Pranav's school context influences his perceptions of the government-endorsed textbooks and his pedagogical choices when teaching English. The private single-sex boy's confessional secondary school, founded during colonial rule, is recognised for its impeccable reputation for catering to the holistic development of its students. The vision and mission of the college nurture the emotional, spiritual and physical emancipation of the students, whilst ensuring academic brilliance. The level of healthy academic and athletic competition is high, and both academic and athletic performance ranges from good to excellent as per national statistics. Students have intermediate to advanced levels of English proficiency as per CEFF levels and attaining A* to C credits at SC level is the norm (MES statistics, 2018–2023). As from Grade 8, classes are streamed according to academic performance.

During the initial interview, Pranav spent considerable time discussing the context of his school detailing how academic excellence is nurtured from the onset of Grade 7 and how the school is in the top tier despite not specialising as an academy. He details how different stakeholders (school management, Heads of Departments [HODs], teachers, The Parents Teaching Association [PTA], parents and students) strive to work hard to maintain academic excellence. In this milieu, Pranav specifies how school management and HODs regulate the school curriculum at their level.

Although the school follows the Nine Year Continuous Basic Education reform (NYCBE) (2016) and students sit for the National Certificate of Education (NCE) at the end of the lower secondary cycle at Grade 9, the school maintains a degree of autonomy in their operationalisation. One of the most significant decisions is to ensure that teachers use a variety of prescribed textbooks they consider useful, alongside the MIE Ministry-endorsed textbooks. Pranav discusses how school management and the head of department consider the level and content of the Ministry-endorsed government-endorsed textbooks to be "too basic" [DI:23] and not "challenging" [DI:20] enough for the students at the college. More importantly, Pranav discusses at length how the head of department and colleagues do not feel that the MIE government-endorsed English textbooks have sufficient content to prepare their students for the high-stake NCE examinations and how the "activities are not exam-oriented" [DI:17].

T: [I]t [Communication skills] should be, but our current education system doesn't cater for like communication skills, like skills exams, for example. It is only at form 5 level that we have oral exams. It's good that we prepare them from Grade 7, but the students at times, feel, it's useless.

Pranav is adamant that the level of the English textbooks is not suitable for secondary school students whose English proficiency ranges from intermediate to advanced. For example, he believes that the Grade 7 English textbook is "more like Grade 5" [DI:75-76], meaning that it is more in line with upper primary level. Pranav, firmly, believes that the Ministry-endorsed English textbooks should be more exam-oriented and should not focus so much on the communicative aspect of English.

The above vignette is significant for several reasons. Firstly, it accentuates that Pranav's English teaching orientation is fundamentally of a traditional exam-orientated nature and despite doing a PGCE in English which caters for the functional and communicative use of the language and challenges the status quo of teaching for exams, his own views of why students study English is more rigid. Although he acknowledges that communicative skills are important for functional purposes, he does not deem these important skills to be developed as there is a lack of exam focus at NCE level on these skills. He also appears to have an insider's knowledge of his students' view of communicative skills and thinks that his students do not like working on these skills. However, deeper analysis hints that his own actions may well promote and foster this feeling in his students or from another angle, it may be that his own perceptions are being superimposed on his students.

As the government-endorsed English textbooks are part and parcel of the resources to be used in the implementation stage of the NYCBE reform (2016), Pranav feels forced and accountable to use the textbooks as "it is imposed by the Ministry" [DI:84]. If he had full teacher autonomy, Pranav shares that he would not use the government-endorsed textbooks. However, Pranav is not completely negative about the content of the English textbooks. For example, he believes that the reading passages are well-prepared and, according to him, are in line with the NCE exam requirements. He, even, suggests that he would advise newly recruited colleagues to use the reading units for "drill"[DI:56]. Nonetheless, Pranav remains sceptical about the writing activities highlighting what he perceives to be a lack of scope for development. For example, he pinpoints a specific creative writing activity in the Grade 7 textbook which focuses on a superhero's adventure where students have to complete a comic strip. Pranav is critical of this activity as in his view,

T: it [comic strip] does not match what is expected for exams, like for example, a student, can only write, uh, one sentence in one, how do you say that? Dialogue box. In an essay, there will be a flow. They will need to know how to write it, how to make it flow, instead of only one sentence. They will have to write in paragraphs and have their story flow.

This vignette reiterates Pranav's traditional views of teaching English which does not focus on developing the creativity of his students.

In contrast to his negative perception of the government-endorsed textbooks, it is interesting to note how Pranav upholds similar views as his colleagues from the Department of English and how he, too, valorises international English textbooks from South-Asian countries. According to Pranav, the content level of these international English textbooks aligns with the level and needs of students from his college. Along with his colleagues, Pranav opines that these international textbooks cater for the functional purpose of preparing students for reading, writing and grammar.

4.4.2 Pranav's Pedagogical Choices in Using Government-Endorsed Textbooks

During the lesson observations, it was interesting to note that Pranav chooses only reading and writing activities from the textbooks and skips the communication activities that build on the listening and speaking skills of the learners as it is not part of the Grades 7 and 8 internal assessment and Grade 9 NCE examinations. Pranav explains how, along with his colleagues, they "don't put emphasis on communication skills for exams, so we tend to discard that" and then he proceeds to list superficial technical reasons why he prefers not to teach speaking and listening skills on the grounds that "there is lack of equipment".

It is interesting to note the pedagogical choices that Pranav makes when teaching reading, writing and grammar to Grades 7 and 8 students. For example, during the Grade 7 lesson observation class, which was a reading comprehension on *Animal Cruelty*, Pranav follows the activities in the textbook with some changes. For instance, for the pre-reading activity which is a think-pair-share oral activity with pictures as triggers, he requests them to "reflect and write their answers in their exercise books" and proceeds by asking the class to share their responses. Depending on the answers, Pranav prompts students further. When one student answers "[t]hey [people] abuse animals", Pranav asks "for what purpose?". For the while-reading activity, the main difference in teaching is that he asks different students to read paragraphs. He, then, proceeds to use the paraphrastic approach and he requests them to explain the paragraph in French before proceeding to the comprehension questions in the textbook, which students do individually.

Similarly, for the writing activity for another Grade 7 class, he adheres to the activities found in the textbook with some clarification given on what students need to do. In contrast, when teaching active and passive voice to lower-stream Grade 8 students, although Pranav started with the grammar activity in the English language textbook, when students struggled and asked for further clarification, he asked them to refer to the notes that he had given them on direct and indirect speech and asked them to revise. He provided some explanation about how some of the tenses change but when students continued to struggle, he reiterated the need to revise the notes and gave them a series of drills from the international South-Asian textbook to do as homework.

4.4.3 Analysis

Interpretation of the findings indicates that Pranav's teacher cognition (beliefs, attitudes and identity) shapes his pedagogical choices. From Pranav's perspective, the teaching of English is not for enjoyment, functional and communicative purposes. Instead, teaching English *should* be exam-oriented, and students *should* practise English drill exercises to excel at examinations. Deeper interpretation reveals that although Pranav did a PGCE at the Mauritius Institute of Education (MIE) with several colleagues who conceptualised the English textbooks and who put forward a more inductive, integrated and students-needs approach to teaching English, Pranav does not endorse this and moves away from such orientation. In other words, his orientation to English language teaching stems from his own set of beliefs and from the context that he works in. Going even deeper, it may be interpreted that these beliefs are entrenched in his own experience as a student at the school where he now works.

Analysis of Pranav's pedagogical choices and his teaching strategies reveal that he embraces detailed activities in textbooks, which at surface level, do not require a substantial amount of teacher preparation and intervention when teaching to proficient classes. This explains why Pranav, further, embraces the reading and writing activities in the government-endorsed textbooks which are detailed and require minimum intervention from him when teaching to students with good to excellent English proficiency levels. Pranav does not endorse the grammar activities in the government-endorsed English textbooks because they do not follow the traditional deductive rules-based and drill format that he favours. The grammar activities in the government-endorsed textbooks are task-based and inductive and often require additional teacher support and scaffolding depending on the level of proficiency of students. Embracing a traditional grammar orientation, Pranav believes that students should be given rule-based notes to revise and learn and then practice drills for perfection. This entails additional teacher preparation, and when students struggle with understanding as evidenced in the Grade 8 grammar lesson, it seems that Pranav is unsure how to clarify their confusion and provide pedagogical support. This raises questions about Pranav's Pedagogical Content Knowledge (PCK) and whether he is apt to help students, and it may explain why he prefers international South-Asian textbooks which provide detailed rule-based explanations and a series of drill exercises. From the interviews and observations conducted, it can be interpreted that his insecurity about his proficiency in English governed his pedagogical choices and these were also part and parcel of his teacher self, his teacher cognition as well as agency.

4.5 Rabiah: The Defensive Driver

This case study explores Rabiah's perspectives and practices regarding textbook use in her English language classroom. The study is based on an analysis of interview data and classroom observations, highlighting the teacher's strategies, content coverage and use of various resources.

Rabiah considers herself to be a novice teacher, with only about 3 years of teaching experience. After her degree in English at the University of Mauritius, she completed her MA as well as a Postgraduate Certificate in London. She, then, joined the education sector as a supply teacher in a State School, and enrolled on a PGCE course at the MIE. While she was still following that course, she joined a private confessional college as English teacher, which is where this case study is set.

4.5.1 Perceptions of the Textbook

Rabiah has mixed feelings about the government-endorsed textbooks. Her school has recently started using the MIE textbooks, and so far, she has used the Grade 7 and Grade 9 English textbooks. These, however, are often complemented with grammar textbooks such as Alter, Hammond and L.B. Clarks. On this account, she finds that her school grants her that flexibility to work with more than one textbook:

T: No, actually, the school gives us this flexibility to change textbook. We don't stick to one. And actually it also depends on the needs of the learners. So, for example, if they need more drills? We'll give it to them. If they need more passages like the one that I did, so I would then use the MIE textbook. I would not restrict myself to one.

She finds that some of the content of these grammar textbooks are very useful, especially since she finds the Grade 9 textbook either does not cover some grammar items in depth, or if it does, then only vaguely. She perceives these grammar books as a valuable resource and appreciates the amount of detail as well as the instructions that come in the grammar books. However, she notes that these books could be used more frequently and strategically to complement the mainstream textbook. On another note, she does select which passages to teach from the MIE textbook, as evidenced by the interview extract below:

I: So, do you do all the components?
R: No, I do skip the components ... that's because there are some passages that students are not really interested, so I have to skip them or I have to adapt. I have to bring, Uh, topic of interest for them. Otherwise they will be like, bored.

As example, Rabiah cites the 'Going Green' Unit from the Grade 7 textbook, which she had to rework as a project given her students could not process a big chunk of text presented in the textbook. Rabiah, thus, customises her use of the textbook to cater for her learners and tries to ensure that their learning needs come first, rather than fulfilling a programmatic need to implement the NYCBE curricular reform.

4.5.2 *Rabiah's Pedagogical Choices in Using Government-Endorsed Textbooks*

Rabiah emphasises the importance of thorough lesson planning, stating, "I got my lesson plan ready. ... I had to know what to first and then how to get the responses from my students". Lesson sequencing is not strictly linear, with Rabiah incorporating activities not directly linked to the textbook. Brainstorming sessions and discussions are used to supplement the textbook content and make connections between different parts of the lesson. One example of this is when Rabiah uses brainstorming to generate ideas about the consequences of climate change, which are, then, supplemented with specific examples from the textbook:

T: So for example, if you remember, there was this 'consequences ' part. Like the consequence of climate change. Like we went to the textbook. And the textbook gave us specific examples. I think many animals, they left their habitat and go. So this is one example of the consequence that the students ... I think they could not be specific about it. But then they got the answer from the textbook. Lifted this and we posted it on the whiteboard. [...] It was not linear. It was there, the ideas that we could gather, on the board so that it makes sense to the students. Like they could see. These are causes, consequences, solutions.

Such preparation also includes conducting research and anticipating what and how her students would respond to maintain their interest and engagement. She recognises the significance of personal enthusiasm and setting up a conducive classroom atmosphere in facilitating student interest.

When it comes to the coverage of the content, Rabiah acknowledges the National Curriculum Framework (NCF) as a guiding document for her pedagogical choices and teaching moves. However, her more immediate frame of reference remains the textbooks and the examinations, which enable her to map out what needs to be covered throughout the year. Rabiah follows a structured approach, ensuring that grammar topics are consistently addressed while allowing for some flexibility when it comes to comprehension and essay writing activities. Even then, she finds that the exercises proposed in the MIE textbooks tend to be limited and she, thus, complements with exercises derived either from the Internet or from grammar-specific textbooks:

T: no actually I would like the paper to resemble the book. I would love more activities, exercises which I find a bit lacking in the textbook … such as … Let's say for example, the one that I am telling you. Direct and indirect speech. I think this is the only example that I can take. I think it from the Grade 8 textbook … and that exercise is only one page. Well, there's not an exercise. There's just like … I think few sentences and you just have to observe the inverted commas. Yeah. That's the thing. And then when we had the sample paper from the MES, we had one exercise where the students were asked to put this indirect speech into direct speech. So, then how would they do this if … I know the teacher has to complement the textbook. But then it's not even this exercise. Does not even have a follow up in the Grade 9 textbook. It's only one page as if it's insignificant and that exercise is one or two marks in the grammar section.

Rabiah does not always follow the textbook chronologically, but rather selects units and activities based on her students' needs and prior knowledge. For instance, she prioritises the coverage of literature and stylistic devices as her students have not yet covered those topics by the time she had joined this school.

Before delving into comprehension passages, Rabiah prioritises brainstorming exercises. This helps her gauge her students' prior knowledge and address any misconceptions that may arise, while also enhancing student participation and interest in the subsequent reading comprehension. She prefers this kind of engagement with the text to traditional methods that usually involve the students reading aloud the text.

Rabiah acknowledges the need for explicit vocabulary instruction, particularly in comprehension exercises. This aims to enhance students' understanding of the text and expand their vocabulary. When preparing for lessons, Rabiah anticipates vocabulary challenges and identifies words that students may not know. This allows her to pre-empt, explain these terms and ensure students can fully engage with the textbook content. **She, also, consistently checks for prior knowledge, as evidenced by the review of past tense verbs observed at the beginning of a lesson. This practice helps to reinforce previously learned material and prepare her students for new content.**

Rabiah employs a combination of open-ended and targeted questions to elicit student responses and encourage participation in class. She, also, uses prompts and scaffolding techniques to support their understanding, often translating **into their mother tongue, KM,** when necessary:

T: Now let's take a look at this recipe. Sa veut dire quoi recipe?
S: *recette.*
T: recette. Exactly. Let us take a look at the recipe and the ingredients that we need to bake the cake. Okay. Huh, Ryan? Could you read the recipes for me please? The ingredients, sorry. What do we need? 1 … Cup? *Ki li bzn pour faire recette la? Pour faire gateau la?* Yes? Sorry? [Student answers] oui, how much? How many? 1 cup Oates. What does Oates mean? Oatmeal. Oat veut dire oatmeal. Dakore? Cereal. Dakore? Après, what do we need more? Huh, Michael? What do we need more? [Student answers] yogurt. What is yogurt? [Student answers] *yaourt.* Okay. How many cup do we need? [Student answers] one. yes. Après, *ki nou bzn? Ethan?* [Student answers] grated? Grated, *sa veut dire koi grated?* [Student answers] *raper.* Sa veut dire, we have to grape. … How many apples? [Student answers] 2 apples. Humm, I can see that this is going to be a very good cake la ein. Because, we have Oates, we have yogurt. We have apples. And

what more do we need matadeen? [Student answers] canola oil. Saveut dire sa c 1 type de? [student answers] de huile. Cacoa non. [Laughs] [Student answers] exactly. You are going to see in a minute la ein. Where we are going to use that. Okay. Après what do we need, my friend, here? Après de huile, what do we need?

She finds that with some activities in the textbook, she has to use the classroom space and physical demonstrations to illustrate concepts such as prepositions. This interactive approach helps her students to visualise and internalise the meaning of these terms. In a similar vein, she incorporates pictures and real-world objects into her teaching, moving beyond the textbook's suggested resources. Visuals, such as cartoons and drawing activities, help to enhance student interest and focus. This strategy, she explains, helps to make the content she has to teach more relatable and engaging to students. She, however, acknowledges potential challenges in implementing these strategies, such as her students' varying abilities at drawing, which may make them reluctant to engage in these activities. While Rabiah finds the textbook to be a valuable resource, she often adapts and supplements it with additional materials and activities to cater to her students' specific needs and interests. She, thus, shows some degree of flexibility and responsiveness in her use of textbooks in her English classroom:

T: I always do that. I do the 'quiz thing' in the middle. I do the quiz and then we start again and then if I feel that, uh, they are getting too bored, so I would then take the class in the next session. I don't do like a complete whole literature class; no. I have to do some activities.
[Extracted from Interview]

For instance, Rabiah often uses handouts and worksheets, including those with pictures, to supplement textbook materials. Those worksheets are, sometimes, sourced or adapted from online sources, particularly ESL worksheets and offer scaffolded activities that cater to different student levels to ensure that her students are learning in a supportive environment. **These handouts help in her teaching of vocabulary and provide additional practice for different grammatical items in a more gradual way than the MIE textbooks allow her to do:**

> And, I also get my worksheets from ESL lessons online. Uh, because … the activities they are very scaffolded, that is, they start very easy and then you choose level 1, level 2, level 3 … so it depends. First I will choose the level one and I see how it … did they master the rule? Did they understand the rule? So, if I give them the worksheet and I see that there are mistakes, errors, they haven't understood at all, so then I will take away the worksheet and then we are going to do explanation, brainstorming again etcetera, then I will then give it to them again.

Rabiah, generally, finds the pictures and graphics in the MIE textbooks to be clear and helpful in illustrating concepts. However, she, also, supplements by looking for additional related images, videos and songs which are aligned to the themes in the textbook and might enhance student engagement and confidence in English, thus eliciting more responses from her students.

R: You can just tell me what you prepared. Now in the textbook, here we can see that there is a teaching tip which is to use a box and a bowl. What did you use instead of this?
T: well, I did this one.
R: the worksheet. So the worksheet used pictures.
T: yeah, and then I used the students themselves. And I used realias like hands on thing like marker, book,
R: things which are visible 'in front of' them.

She, also, sometimes adapts textbook questions to better suit her students' abilities, often starting with lower-order thinking questions before progressing to higher-order ones. **She, also, effectively uses the board to emphasise the teaching of key vocabulary and concepts and reinforce student learning through visual representation.** Rabiah believes that this approach promotes inclusivity and allows all students to participate. In addition, she finds that integrating project work (e.g., on the 'Going Green' Unit in Grade 7) fosters rapport and enhances learning. She complements these pedagogical choicess with quizzes and group activities to maintain her students' interest. In the following extract from an observation of her class, Rabiah can be seen engaging her students in miming the action of mixing ingredients. These kinds of simulated exercises are, in her view, very effective at engaging the learners she, currently, has since they transform a potentially static reading exercise in the textbook into something they can all imagine and enact:

T: so, can we all take out our books and copybooks?
S: yes.
T: what is this other word for excited that we learnt? Starting with 'd'?
S: delighted
T: delighted. Yes. You do remember. Okay, girls. You know today, I am very hungry. And I didn't have breakfast. So today, you will help me to bake a cake. So, you need to open your book on page 164. 164 [in creole] [waits for students] okay? All of you have …? [Organizes students seating, sets them in pairs] let us now take a look at the pictures. *Nou get 1 cout ban foto*. The pictures that we can see in the book. Let's take a look at the pictures. Ryan, page 164? Yes? So, I will give you one minute to take a look at the pictures. Après, you will tell me what you see in the pictures. [Directed to student] yes Govin, you can have water. [Back to class] the picture in the book. [Directed to student] Hans, are you having a look at the pictures in your book? Okay. I am going to ask you what you can see. Yes? [Directed to student] are you having a look at the pictures? [Checking students individually] you are going to learn about these words. Okay? Now, let's take a look at the last picture. *Derniere photo*. Last picture. What do you see?
S: a cake.
T: it is a cake. It is a bit like a cupcake. Have you ever tried a cupcake?
S: yes.
T: okay. Was that a good experience? *Comment experience a eter?*
[T initiates miming and role play based on the activity]
T: Hans can you mix the mixture now? What do we have? A mixture. c'est quoi mixture? Savedire aprer add, we have 'mix'. Mix the ingredients [writes on board] une fois ki noun funi melanger. We have a mixture. What do we do now? Before adding in the tray? Before pouring in the tray. [Student answers] nou geter sipa Lin bien craser. Yes. Après?
S: met duberre dans … Butter.
T: how do we call that? Alle Hans, grease the tray. Greasing the tray [writes on board] once we have grease the tray, what do we do? Yes matadeen? You pour the mix. … The mix ou the mixture? The mixture, melange.

4.5.3 Analysis

Rabiah's pedagogical choices in using the government-endorsed textbooks to teach English, are deeply intertwined with her beliefs, knowledge and experiences. Several factors were noted to have impacted on her textbook usage. Firstly, she adapts her practices to cater to her students' level and motivation. Recognising her students' limited exposure to, and proficiency in, the English language, she moves to and from in her use of the different languages in her class, often translating instructions in Kreol Morisien, and providing explicit feedback to bridge the gap between her students' linguistic abilities and the language of the textbook. The choice of language also varies depending on the grade level and proficiency of the students. She uses a mix of English and Kreol Morisien with Grade 7 students, while encouraging Grade 9 students to communicate predominantly in English. **There is, hence, an implicit understanding of sociocultural theories of learning that emphasise social interaction and language in knowledge construction, overriding the need to implement, then, the NYCBE reform This is what guides most of her pedagogical choices and moves.**

While acknowledging the value of the textbook as a structured resource, Rabiah, actively, supplements it with various strategies and materials to enhance student engagement and learning outcomes. This adaptability demonstrates a student-centred approach, where the teacher prioritises meeting the diverse needs of their learners over strict adherence to the textbook's methods.

Her emphasis on brainstorming and activating prior knowledge aligns with constructivist learning theories, which posit that students learn best by building upon their existing knowledge and experiences. By eliciting students' thoughts and ideas before introducing new material, she creates a more relevant and meaningful learning experience. Moreover, her use of demonstrations, realia, visuals and kinaesthetic activities (such as role-plays) reflects a multi-sensory approach to teaching. This approach caters to different learning styles and helps students grasp abstract concepts through concrete experiences. The incorporation of technology, such as videos and online worksheets, further demonstrates Rabiah's commitment to using diverse resources to enhance learning. Her decision to supplement the MIE textbooks with worksheets, quizzes and realia stems from her belief that a single textbook cannot fully address the diverse needs of her learners, in line with the standpoint that knowledge is actively built through interaction with the environment. As she tries to diversify resources, Rabiah aims to create more engaging and interactive learning experiences and to cater to different learning styles and preferences.

Rabiah's decision-making processes and beliefs about teaching and learning are evident in her pedagogical choices. Her belief in the importance of explicit vocabulary instruction and scaffolding, for instance, is reflected in their practice of pre-teaching vocabulary and providing ample support to students during comprehension exercises. The teacher's willingness to adapt textbook questions and activities to align with their students' levels indicates a strong awareness of learner differences and a commitment to inclusive practices. This adaptability suggests a reflective practitioner who continuously assesses student needs and adjusts their teaching accordingly. Furthermore, Rabiah's use of the mother tongue as a scaffolding tool reflects an understanding of the importance of linguistic and cultural context in language learning. By bridging the gap between students' first language and the target language, the teacher facilitates comprehension and empowers students to express themselves more confidently. Although Rabiah espouses not concurring with much of the philosophy that guides the NYCBE reform and the government endorsed textbooks, she enacts the curricular reform in her practice, unconsciously, through the learner-centred pedagogy she proposes for her students. Her teacher agency, whilst being strong, rides the current of the NYCBE reform.

4.5.4 Noted Challenges and Limitations

This case study, also, highlights several challenges and limitations that Rabiah experienced while using the MIE textbooks. The teacher identifies issues such as the lack of grammar activities, the fact that some exercises were decontextualised and were not more interactive and engaging. Those limitations highlight the teacher's perception that the textbook, while valuable, is not entirely suitable to her specific teaching context.

At the same time, Rabiah acknowledges that contextual and institutional factors impact on her pedagogical choices. For instance, she admits that the lack of reading culture and time constraints due to a heavy workload require her to modify her approach to her textbook usage. While there is flexibility to work with more than one textbook, there is, however, the implicit pressure **to adhere to the MIE textbook due to its perceived alignment with the national examinations. Such pressure significantly limits her autonomy and flexibility in adapting the textbook**

to better suit her students' needs. Prioritising exam preparation leads her to focus on specific skills and content areas which might not be fully aligned with the textbook's structure or her students' interests. **As a novice teacher, Rabiah also feels challenged by a lack of comprehensive training in textbook adaptation, and she has to rely on her own resourcefulness and initiative to supplement the textbook effectively.**

4.5.5 Conclusion

These case studies reveal the ways the participants of this study perceived and used the government endorsed textbooks in their English language classroom. Their cognitive processes and beliefs as well as their teacher agency about teaching and learning play a crucial role in shaping their instructional practices. This study uncovers the complex interplay between the teacher's practices, beliefs and the institutional context in which they operate. Their use of the textbook is not merely a matter of following guidelines, but is also a dynamic process of adaptation, supplementation and strategic decision-making based on their knowledge and the specific needs of their students. These case studies emphasis teacher agency and adaptability in maximising the effectiveness of the government endorsed textbooks. It underscores the need to acknowledge and address the challenges of mandated textbooks, empowering teachers to use them flexibly. By viewing the textbook as a starting point rather than a rigid script, teachers like most of our participants show that they can create more engaging, relevant and inclusive learning experiences and enact, adapt or reject the curricular reform through the pedagogical choices informing the use of the government-endorsed textbooks.

REFERENCES

Baleghizadeh, S., & Dargahi, Z. (2016). What aspects of creativity enhancement do ELT textbooks take into account? In *SLA research and materials development for language learning* (pp. 185–197). Routledge.

Tomlinson, B. (2015). Challenging teachers to use their coursebook creatively. In A. Maley & N. Peachey (Eds.), *Creativity in the English language classroom* (pp. 24–28). British Council.

CHAPTER 5

Curricular Reform in a SIDS: Teacher Cognition and Teacher Agency Locking the Brakes to Curricular Reform

Abstract This chapter synthesises the findings of the case studies, offering an in-depth analysis of the pedagogical choices made by teachers when using the government endorsed MIE textbooks, designed, conceptualised and written by minority textbook writers. It, critically, examines the perceptions of teachers on the textbook, exploring how these perceptions influence their pedagogical choices. The chapter also links the emergent themes from the case studies to the existing literature, providing a deeper understanding of textbook use in the Mauritian context, as well as situating minority textbook writers' cognition, beliefs and philosophies as another expanse of research area that demands more scrutiny.

Keywords Dissonance • Criticism • Exam-driven • Teacher agency • Teacher cognition • Pedagogical choices

5.1 Orientation

This chapter ties in the findings of the study with an in-depth analysis, exploring the pedagogical choices made by teachers when using the government-endorsed English textbooks in their classes. It seeks to bring forth possible interpretations to understanding the data. It does so by linking the data represented in the case studies and offering a comparative critical analysis of the perceptions of the teachers on the textbook as well as their pedagogical choices, seeking to best understand *how* the perceptions influence the pedagogical choices made and *why* these choices are made. In the bigger backdrop, it then extends the analysis to shed light on how teachers, in a small island developing state, enact or resist curricular reform in their classes.

This chapter will be divided into several sections organised into different analytical categories. The first section will draw out a comparison between the perceptions of the four participants on the textbooks. The section on perceptions leads us to the main theme that emerges from the findings of the research that we conducted: that teachers' perceptions are driven by their *teacher cognition*. The second section looks at ***how their teacher cognition informs their teacher agency*** and the pedagogical choices that they make when they use the government-endorsed textbooks. Following the setting up of the possible interpretations in this chapter, the analysis will be further abstracted to a theoretical dimension where the emergent themes of the different case studies will be discussed in the light of the existent literature in the last section of this chapter.

5.2 Teacher Cognition: Teachers' Perceptions of Government-Endorsed English Textbooks

As minority textbook writers, when we started the project and data production, we stepped in the field with the belief that most schools would be using the textbooks we had conceptualised, designed and written, given that it was recommended by the Ministry and endorsed by the government, in the context of the curricular reform. We were, thus, surprised by the fact that several academically reputed "schools [had totally ***scrapped] the MIE textbooks to actually choose other textbooks***" as they felt that they were not useful to prepare their students for the different gateway examinations. Our participants have mixed feelings about the government-endorsed textbooks and perceptions and their pedagogical **choices to use them** vary according to their teacher cognition and agency. Whilst some, like Pranav, feel that there is no choice but to use the textbook and argue that "it has been imposed" by the Ministry and authorities, others, like Rabiah, do not feel the compulsion of using it since they have the freedom to complement the usage of the textbook with other textbooks and resources. However, despite this individual freedom, Rabiah is quick to point out that there is a strong belief amongst some of her colleagues that the government-endorsed textbooks, even if considered as limited, should not be ignored as it is endorsed by the Ministry of Education and provided freely to teachers and students. As a newcomer to her current school, Rabiah is, thus more circumspect in her approach towards textbooks, whether they are from MIE or from other sources. In contrast, Reema, who has been advised by her head of the department not to use the textbook in her classes, bypasses the authority of her head and chooses to make use of the government textbooks at the various levels she is teaching. She, firmly, believes that the end of year gateway NCE (National Certificate of Education) examinations will be dictated by the curricular reform and the textbooks lead to the acquisition of competencies, skills and attitudes requisite for the assessment changes that will happen due to the curricular reform.

However, one of the main findings of this study is that perceptions of Mauritian teachers are shaped by their grammar-centric teaching philosophy. Due to this belief, most feel that segments of the textbooks are not aligned with the teaching purposes that they might have as most teachers are concerned by **the teaching of grammar**. Thus, most of them found that the activities proposed by the textbook **are not sufficient for the teaching of grammar**. This is, further, reiterated by Pranav, who teaches at an urban private confessional college. He believes that there are not enough grammar activities, and he repeats this several times, stating that the textbook should have "more activities ... like more work, worksheets, work, more grammar exercises" and that "practice makes perfect". This underscores his belief that English language teaching is more do with the practice of grammar activities. Rabiah also believes the government-endorsed textbook to be limited, and she supplements it with at least two grammar books (Alter and Hammond) as well as notes from the Internet. This ties in with the different studies done on textbook writing in various contexts, showcasing clearly that teachers are very much in control of how they choose to use any textbook, whether they are part of a curricular reform or not. We note in our study that the teachers, who were our participants, were very much resistant to the grammar teaching philosophy that were embedded within the textbooks we conceptualised, designed and wrote where emphasis was laid on the concrete use of grammar rather than isolating grammatical items, drilling and 'rote learning' of grammatical items. This already sets up the *dissonance that exists between the drivers of the curricular reform, the teachers and the engineers of the curricular reform, the <u>minority textbook writers that we are.</u>*

Concurring with the literature that was reviewed, we found that the participants of this study felt that the textbook designed was not appropriate for the level of the students they teach. Whilst some feel that it is too high level for their students, some feel that the level is not adequate for high-level students. Reema, who was based in an urban private-aided school, claims that "the level is high. Because, like, today when we did the theatre one, the kids didn't understand the passage at all". She, further, added that "there are some things that are a bit too difficult for the kids". On the other hand, Pranav clearly stated that the textbooks for Grades 7 to 9 are not up to the level and need to be more challenging in terms of content. He asserted that the textbooks are flimsy even for the lower streams and considers the textbook to be of primary level material. In Rabiah's teaching context, where she often must deal with struggling students, this means that she either must "adapt or skip sections of the textbook" which might be too challenging for her students. Eventually, she finds herself being an intermediary or a translator between the textbook and her students and she must deploy several strategies to ensure that her students understand what is required of them.

It was also noted that most teachers felt that some sections of the textbook were redundant and most of our participants ended up not using them. This view is echoed by Rabiah, who believed that the textbook should be able to better prepare both teacher and students for examinations. She found that the smaller tasks presented in the textbook do not necessarily "prepare the student to develop essay writing skills", for instance. Similarly, Vedi confirmed that she taught the "oral" component lesser "(b)ecause (she) find(s) it comes along with the reading comprehension itself, it is already there, so they are already reading". Reema, on the other hand, adapted the different activities proposed by the textbook to suit her teaching purpose. Hence, she clearly stated that she did not use the books "completely" as she does not "compartmentalise". She could, thus, make use of a reading text given to teach comprehension to give a "test" and "give them an appeal of working a comprehension in 10 minutes because for the exams". Whilst she was correcting, she also uses the text available to teach grammar side by side. She, therefore, amalgamated the usage of the textbook to suit her teaching style as also meet her objectives set out for her teaching.

The participants of this study, hence, found it challenging to use the textbook for diverse reasons. Rabiah, for instance, felt that she always had "to do some extra" as it lacked practice exercises. She believed that the textbook writers could have added more "interactive activities for students" but however recognised that what would work in her current school might not necessarily be appropriate in another school context, where perhaps "we need more drills and exercises ... which are absent in the [MIE] book". While she appreciated textbooks that offer such exercises, she realised that this would have alienated some of her former students who needed more motivating and contextually apt content. Rabiah also pointed out that her friends who were teachers in other schools sometimes reject the MIE textbook. This concurred with the existent literature where curricular reform carried out in other diverging contexts abroad met with resistance on the part of the drivers of curricular reform. This is due to their teaching philosophy which is guided by their major concern, namely, the exams. **This holds true for Mauritius, where *we, as minority textbook writers, juggled with our own teaching and learning philosophy which was embedded in the conceptualisation, design and writing of the Grade 7-9 textbooks which met with resistance to curricular reform due to the strong teacher cognition and agency. The curriculum designers were principally guided by the NCF and the Teaching and Learning Syllabus. Hence, the textbooks aimed at teaching the different language skills; namely communication skills, reading and writing, integrating the teaching of vocabulary and grammar within the teaching of these skills. Emphasis was laid on the teaching and learning of the language competencies, attitudes and behaviour and hence, the textbooks offer a wide range of interactive and learner-centered activities. The use of learner-centered approaches was favoured to guide the teaching/learning of English and one of the key aims when designing and writing the textbooks was to ensure that learners were unable and writing the textbooks was to ensure that learners were able to use English with growing proficiency.***

Derisively, so, we understood through the research conducted that teachers were governed more by their traditional grammar-centred teaching philosophy, and they felt that the exams were more grammar-centric than skills-based, so this only served to reinforce their own ***teacher cognition*** and brought in the resistance we met with at any curricular reform we conceptualised of.

5.2.1 The Impact of Exam-Centric Teaching Philosophy on Curricular Reform

Most of the teachers' perceptions of the textbooks were informed by the importance the exams had and their teaching is shaped by their exam-centric teaching philosophy. We have diverging views concerning the perceptions of our participants about the English Grades 7 to 9 language textbooks and whether they are appropriate and suitable to prepare students for the exams. Consequently, Pranav vehemently argued that "the activities are not exam-centred" and that teachers "cannot only be dependent on THAT book!" and suggested that "another textbook in parallel" be used. He further expounded that "I would use the creole term *comblage* when we have some **free time** in our English period, then we might use the English, the MIE textbook". He firmly believed that the government-endorsed English textbooks were not exam-oriented. He was most critical of the creative writing activities in the MIE textbook as he felt that they did not prepare students for exam-based questions. On the other hand, Reema believed that the textbook was important as it developed the different competencies that are a prerequisite for the national exams and she stated that she wanted "them to have a feel of the different types of passages because we have no clue as teachers, what's coming for the exams". She, therefore, felt that the government-endorsed MIE textbooks were going to impact on the setting of the national exams and claimed that "[t]he reason being that the exams are going to be similar, if not, exactly the same as MIE".

Rabiah believed that there should be a strong correlation between the textbook structure and content and the Grade 9 examination paper. She felt that going through the textbook with her students conditioned them to think of language exercises in a certain way; for instance, in "the textbook, we've got a lot of pictures but in the exam paper, there are not many pictures", and this can "put off students". While she would like a paper that "resembles the book", she still "would love more activities, exercises, which [she] finds a bit lacking in the textbook", especially since she feels that "giving [students] the book and asking them to do the activity only, like text, and then written exercise, this would not work".

Rabiah felt that the government-endorsed MIE textbook presents a steep learning curve for her students who face numerous challenges as language learners. This means that when she used the textbook in class, she had to break down the different proposed activities into manageable parts and integrate textbook work into a larger lesson that would consist of clearly demarcated stages. She felt that the MIE textbook is "messy" because her students cannot get on board the proposed textbook activities, and that it inevitably entailed considerable reworking at her end. This in turn impacted on the time she felt she should devote to examination preparation, given that her reputation as a teacher is at stake. The success of her students in formal examinations inevitably is deemed to reflect her own efforts as teacher and she wished that the government-endorsed MIE could provide that closer link to what the examination paper would be. *All this only serves to highlight to what extent the exams drive the teaching of our participants and informs their teacher cognition and agency and has an important hand in the driving of any curricular reform.*

5.3 Teacher Agency: Teachers' Pedagogical Choices When Using the Government-Endorsed Textbooks

5.3.1 Teachers' Pedagogical Choices

What comes across clearly from the interpretation of the data produced in the context of this study, is the ***teacher agency*** that informs all the pedagogical practices of our participants. Based on their diverse ***teacher cognition and beliefs***, the teachers amalgamated the use of the government-endorsed textbooks with pedagogical strategies and additional resources to complement their teaching. Hence, we found that most of our participants used the textbooks by adapting the activities to suit their teaching purpose or by extending and supplementing with additional activities, strategies as well as resources.

Most of our participants use ***additional materials, resources or textbooks*** to complement their usage of the MIE Grades 7 to 9 English textbooks. Given that most of them feel that the MIE textbooks are not sufficient to teach grammar, the additional resources are normally geared towards the teaching of grammar, which is the case of Pranav and Rabiah. On the other hand, Reema, who works in an urban private-aided school, uses the activities and texts provided in the MIE Grades 7 to 9 flexibly and adapts them to her teaching purpose. She shows agency by making use of the different activities as well as texts provided to teach for different purposes and by not teaching the activities in the ways proposed by the textbooks and linearly. She also used some of the texts to teach the concept of plot, character, setting and themes which would then serve to consolidate students' writing skills. She also sometimes used reading texts to teach grammar. She also embeds within her teaching the teaching of literature. She, therefore, can use one text for multiple purposes depending on what her teaching objective and target is. Whilst she uses the texts offered for different purposes, she supplements her teaching using PowerPoint presentations which she has prepared in advance.

Rabiah is selective when approaching what is proposed in the MIE textbook. There is an initial appraisal of the content in the book, which she judges with respect to the profile of her students. When the textbook is found to be insufficient, she then adds other resources from the Internet or other sources to provide a more varied experience for the students. Her initial guide in this process is the National Curriculum Framework and the Teaching and Learning Syllabus, in which she grounds her teaching. Rabiah often resorts to the board as a pedagogical resource. She uses it for different purposes, for instance to give out classwork, or highlight a key or challenging word, or to use it as a summary sheet during discussions in the classroom, often translating students' responses (often in Kreol) into English on the board. In the lesson observed below, Rabiah uses the board to recapitulate the different steps in a recipe and uses the board alongside prompting and questioning.

It is clear from the data that the different teachers make the pedagogical choices that cater best for their students' level. For Rabiah, her beliefs about students' level and performance were instrumental in shaping her pedagogical choices. Given she had worked in two schools where students were not considered as "high-flyers", she finds that she could not just implement the textbook in the classroom straight away. Rabiah points out that the relative lack of reading culture in Mauritius greatly impacts students' performance in the English class. In her view, textbooks that provide lengthy passages with "large chunks of readings" would "give the message that it's boring ... and get them demotivated". Having to engage students with such content is thus "a lost battle", which results in her own plan of providing a reworked version of the content and adding additional activities to ensure student interaction and engagement. She thus has "to work on the lesson and maybe choose a topic that is going to grab their attention". In one instance, she mentions that "maybe if I was speaking about the *Avengers*, for example, they would be happier, more engaged ... and it would arrest their attention". Interaction is thus one key concern for Rabiah, who prefers to set tasks based on the textbook and ensure that they are involved in peer correction rather than leaving them to work in isolation on exercises from the textbook because "they have to be active; they can't sit and write".

Students' language proficiency level was a recurrent theme across the interviews with the different participants. Rabiah highlights that every lesson was carefully planned with respect to her students' abilities, and she does not mind the additional time this would take as long as her students could understand what she was trying to teach. Rabiah also points out that she often must think fast to engage her students, many of whom tend to be "energetic" and are likely to "feel bored … if I tell them to sit down and read a text". Moreover, breaking one activity from the textbook into smaller tasks or into project work allows her to keep track of her students' progress. The language Rabiah uses in class while working through the textbook is also significant. She recognises that English is "very foreign" to her students, and while she understands that English is expected to be the medium within the English class, and that the instructions within the textbook are in English, she also points out how "alien" using that language feels to many of her students, even after so many years of schooling. She even points out that some teachers themselves might not be very fluent in the language, which eventually leads to instructions being translated to French or Kreol Morisien. Rabiah thus admits that part of her work is to translate those instructions and much of the content into something comprehensible for her students.

She believes that teaching her students felt "like I had to teach the unknown through the unknown, so it does not quite make sense". One way to build rapport and to instil confidence in her students was using Kreol Morisien in class as foundation, which she then used to bring in English words. She recalls her first days of teaching, when she resorted to English only, until the students told her "Miss, pa pe konpran", and started to rebel against her and even made jokes instead. Rabiah believes that using Kreol Morisien (as well as French) helps her students "grasp the appropriate vocabulary so that they can understand and next time they don't have the same confusion". This has helped her build a rapport with her students since she has adapted to her learners and she recognises that providing feedback in a language that the students can understand can make them feel that "Oh, that was wrong. So, I have to say like this and not like that". She finds that praising the students for trying to use English can reduce their anxiety about using the language.

Similarly, Reema adapts her teaching to ensure that she teaches her students numerous skills so that they can be prepared to sit for exams as she believes that her students' level are not "highflyers". Speaking about their level, she mentions the challenges she faces when teaching them and this has an influence on the different choices that she makes: she, therefore, makes certain pedagogical choices that will cater to her teaching purpose, which is equipping her students with the different skills that will be necessary to sit for the exams. She speaks of the necessity of having to craft her teaching to ensure that they make use of their brains and she does so by devising different strategies and techniques and coming up with additional resources as has been highlighted in Sect. 4.2. The same is noted in the case of Vedi who works in a state school. Given that her students are "highflyers" and she feels that some activities might be limited for them, she adapts her teaching to suit their level.

One of the blatant findings of the study that we conducted, as minority textbook writers, is that teachers depend heavily on resources as the main pedagogical choice and are unable to conceive of a classroom without textbooks or resources for that matter. This aligns with the literature reviewed which has shown that in most ex-British colonies where there has been curricular reform, the textbook is still perceived as being an important tool. Without it, most teachers, pitted in the ***colonial mentality***, cannot function. Such is the case of Mauritian teachers who cannot function without a textbook, even if our findings point to the fact that they resist the NYCBE reform. If we deepen the analysis further and look at the teachers' resistance to curricular reform against the Gramscian lens of hegemony (1971), with hegemony understood as being a logical understanding grounded in a multiplicity of societal forces which favours the status quo, we can further expound that teachers' cognition and agency maintain the status quo of the colonial examination system. It can be argued that teachers are ***colonially subjugated*** (Wa Thiong'o, 1998). They cannot do away without the colonial mentality which guides their cognition, pedagogical choices in the backdrop of a curricular reform and their agency towards the colonial exam system that exists in the SIDS that Mauritius is.

5.3.2 Teacher Cognition and Agency

Teacher cognition shapes teachers' pedagogical choices and affirms their teacher agency. These beliefs range from beliefs about the subject area being taught, the curriculum, the value and usefulness of the textbook and students' profiles, amongst others. As mentioned in the first section, our participants did not find that the textbook that we conceptualised, designed and wrote in light of the NYCBE reform was relevant for their learners' needs and their teaching purposes. For Rabiah, for instance, the textbook was an appropriate representation of the content that needed to be covered from the Teaching and Learning Syllabus, but she did not appreciate the way the content was structured and presented. She felt that the textbook was inadequate in meeting her students' needs. From her perspective, the textbook assumed that the content covered over previous years was already acquired, which was a far cry from the reality she experienced in her classroom. Her students could not recall everything that had been covered unless provided with revision content and strategies. The fact that the government-endorsed MIE textbook presented only negligible revision work and instead introduced new content in a minimal way felt "limited". She, thus, feels compelled to use additional textbooks specialising in grammar, since they provide the much-needed "drills and practice exercises". It could, thus, be surmised that Rabiah wants to make sure that she was addressing the needs of her learners and thus wishes to maximise their chances by using a variety of textbooks and resources. Moreover, speaking from the vantage point of a novice teacher, Rabiah believes that the book did not provide much support for teachers who were new to the profession and who may not know how exactly to proceed with the teaching of certain items, despite some helpful teacher's notes in the textbook.

In Pranav's case, his ingrained notion of how English language should be taught influenced his pedagogical decisions in the classroom. His concern about preparing students to be examination-ready explains his choice of teaching to the exam, which mirrors Rabiah's own pedagogical moves. This entails not covering listening and speaking activities in the Grades 7 and 8 textbooks, as well as not spending too much time on initiating writing activities of a more creative nature. Pranav also demonstrates an ingrained belief that grammar explanations should be given for students to learn through a deductive approach. He is also firmly convinced that drilling is a way to ensure that students know grammar points.

All the participants of the study indicated that they use more than one textbook in class. Rabiah points out at her own agency in her selection of texts as well as in her choice of pedagogy in class. She believes that one textbook can never be enough and that "it will always depend on your learner" and "how the teacher tries to meet the learning objectives by devising and using resources that appeal to the students". With reference to the few schools she has been working in, Rabiah adds that "the textbook that I use there would not be same" if she moved to specific schools given the learners' profiles and needs are "totally different". However, Rabiah does not believe that she must complete all the exercises in the textbook since completing exercises in the textbook is not a guarantee that her students have understood.

From her first school, Rabiah recalls that she was "just given the textbook … and was told that this is going to be my textbook, and I have to use it in class". When she, however, started her PGCE, this is when she learnt to "be flexible with the textbook". She was supported in this learning process by a colleague who told her she could adapt the textbook and that "it's not necessarily that I follow rigidly the textbook", which is something Rabiah has adopted even in her new school. Even though she was not forced to use the MIE textbook in this new environment, she eventually turned to it as the principal text since she felt that "at school, the MIE textbook has become almost a bible". Besides the fact that the books are free and are endorsed by the Ministry of Education, she also believes that the MIE textbook will reflect "whatever there will be in the exam". She still feels that the text was incomplete and potentially boring. She, thus, relies on the Teaching and Learning Syllabus as a guiding document to prepare her scheme of work, choosing which lessons would be more appropriate for her students as per the requirements of the syllabus, and making adaptations or supplementing with other resources instead of chronologically working through the textbook. She also tries to engage her students by using worksheets and quizzes, out of the belief that she "had to vary".

Pranav's actions in terms of the skills that he decides to focus on illustrate his teacher agency. This is clearly shown when he categorically decides not to teach listening and speaking activities, emphasising that, although there are other reasons such as lack of resources, the overriding reason for his pedagogical practices is due to his belief that this textbook does not prepare them for the NCE exams at the end of Grade 9 and that it is a "waste of time".

It can be concluded that teachers' beliefs and understanding of their teaching context shape their pedagogical choices in the backdrop of curricular reform. Their choices are informed by their teacher cognition which is heavily moulded by how the colonial examination system subjugates their mind. Their resistance to using the textbooks conceptualised, designed and written by minority textbook writers serves as a reminder to how strong teacher agency can be in the face of any curricular reform. For any curricular reform to be successful, teachers must be on board and believe in it fully. This is not the case of the teachers in the SIDS (Small Island Developing States) that Mauritius is, and this brings us to our own personal dilemma as minority textbook writers who were the minds behind the curricular reform and led the NYCBE reform by embedding our vision in the textbooks we conceptualised, designed and wrote which were endorsed by the government. This will be taken up in the last chapter of this book as we situate ourselves as minority textbook writers in the continuum that curricular reform is.

Reference

Gramsci, A. (1971). *Selections from the prison notebooks* (Q. Hoare & G. N. Smith, Ed. and Trans.). International Publishers.

Wa Thiong'o, N. (1998). Decolonising the mind. *Diogenes, 46*(184), 101–104.

CHAPTER 6

Minority Textbook Writers' Cognition and Agency

Abstract This chapter discusses the push and pull dynamics that exist between the philosophy underpinning the government endorsed Grades 7-9 MIE English textbooks and the teacher cognition and agency of teachers who use them. The chapter pushes forward the analysis drawn so far to engage in a discussion on textbook conceptualisation, designing and writing by minority textbook writers, as us, the authors of this book. The chapter concludes by mapping out what a complex process any curricular reform is, where the cognition, agency as well as the actions of the different stakeholders do not align.

Keywords Dissonance • Teacher agency • Teacher cognition • Pedagogical choices • Push and pull dynamics • Minority textbook writers

The in-depth analysis of the findings highlights **the *push-and-pull* dynamics that exist between *minority textbook writers' cognition and agency* and *teacher cognition and agency*.** Our teachers had their own perspectives about the government endorsed MIE Grades 7-9 English textbooks and their use of the textbooks was governed by their own teaching philosophy, embodying their teacher cognition and agency. Our participants' views could be summarised to the following opinions; (1) there being not enough grammar activities in the textbook, (2) to the textbooks not being level appropriate and (3) To the textbooks having activities designed that they did not find accessible and reader-friendly and (4) **most importantly, the textbooks being considered inappropriate for the learners as they did not prepare students for the exams.** As was contended in Chap. 1, the conceptualisation, design and writing of the textbooks were underpinned by the **philosophy governing the NYCBE reform**, which was the vision panned out by the government as well as those who conceptualised the curricular reform, through the writing of the NCF as well as the TLS. The lower secondary English textbooks **were conceived to bring forth the philosophy underpinning the curricular reform** and focused on the teaching of the different language skills, namely communication skills, reading and writing whilst integrating the teaching of vocabulary and grammar within the teaching of these skills. Emphasis was laid on the teaching and learning of the language competencies, attitudes and behaviour.

After perusal of our findings, it was clear to us that most of our participants **teach to the exams** and, therefore, **their expectations of what a textbook should look like are governed by the expectation that it should be like the exam paper and this comprises their** *teacher cognition*. Given that most teachers prepare the students to sit for the different exams' exit points, they expect the Grades 7 to 9 English textbooks to cater for this. The paper that is set at the end of the Grade 9 cycle, the National Certificate Exams (NCE), comprises two reading tasks, two writing tasks, a section that tests grammar and the use of English accounting for 35% of the paper and a section that tests literature (MES, 2020). Although, the paper embeds at its crux the same philosophy which runs through "the National Curriculum Framework (NCF) Grades 7, 8 and 9 and the outcomes detailed in the Teaching and Learning Syllabus" (MES, 2020, p. 2), **it is but a summative assessment document and cannot be equated to a textbook**. Its main aim is to test the students at the end of their three years of secondary education, assessing them on the basis of the competencies, attitudes and beliefs taught, acquired and learnt during those three years. As *minority textbook writers who conceived of the NYCBE curricular reform*, the NCF, the TLS as well as the government-endorsed textbooks after numerous and lengthy consultative meetings, *we designed the English language textbooks to cater for the teaching of the necessary competencies, skills and attitudes that could be transferred easily when sitting for the exam paper.*

As was highlighted within the literature, research conducted has shown that teachers use textbooks mainly to prepare students for exam preparation. This study, therefore, aligns with previous research conducted and it is clear in this study that the main concerns of Mauritian teachers are the end-of-year NCE exams. *Expounding our argument further by bringing to it a decolonial lens, as minority textbook writers, we decry the colonial mentality that governs our educational system, where we are unfortunately swimming against the tide, when it comes to our own cognition and agency.* Derisively so, in western contexts, textbooks are frowned upon and are mostly a non-entity as most teachers create their own materials and resources. Issit (2004, p. 683) states:

> The negativity surrounding textbooks in terms of use and status as both literary objects and vehicles for pedagogy is profound. There is a very deep-seated 'anti-textbook ethos' witnessed throughout the education business. This negative view of textbooks is partly informed by a certain professional defensiveness reflecting a contradictory, almost *schizophrenic*,[1] sense of the function and cultural worth of textbooks. Whilst as teaching vehicles textbooks are *scorned by many in the teaching profession as poor and insufficient and as assuming a basically passive learning style*,[2] studies show that they are extensively used—a fact easily confirmed by examination of school budgets as well as by cursory observations of school and university life. Any visitor to the classrooms of mainstream secondary schools in the UK will discover piles of textbooks in various dog-eared states arranged round the sides of rooms.

We cannot but reflect on the outcry of Ngugi when it comes to the **colonised subjugated minds** and **view teacher cognition emanating from our study as being shaped by this subjugation for a colonial examination system that strengthens their agency and confirm their stance towards the NYCBE curricular reform**. Where we take *a very much decolonial stance* to teaching and focus on the acquiring of skills, competencies and attitudes, inspiring ourselves from global curricular reform for our vision, we find that in the end, we are brought back to the colonial subjugated mind against which we can hardly hold our forte. As minority textbook writers also wearing the hat of academics training teachers to teach English at preprimary, primary as well as secondary levels, we

---

[1] Our emphasis.
[2] Our emphasis.

cannot help but reflect on our own cognition, agency and how to situate ourselves in this **push-and-pull dynamics** of curricular reform.[3]

What came out strongly in our study, is that *teachers have agency when it comes to making the choices that they feel suit best their teaching and learning*. Their teacher agency is obviously driven by their teacher cognition. We found that most of our participants reappropriated and adapted the textbooks, showing that they had agency when it came to making pedagogical choices that they felt were right and aligned with their teaching philosophy and suited their teaching purpose. At grassroot level, *teachers do not necessarily stick to the espoused curriculum but instead make pedagogical choices that are grounded in the beliefs they hold and the knowledge they have of their learners and what suits their learners. Their teaching is guided by their beliefs, the knowledge and understanding of their beliefs and their teaching styles and preferences. They do not teach for learning to happen, but they teach to the exams and aim only at getting their students to succeed in the exams.* We highlight this in this book, by **filling the gap on minority textbook writers' cognition and agency**, situated in a SIDS country, with the backdrop of twenty-first-century guided curricular reform. We state that in the face of the NYCBE curricular reform or any curricular reform, **minority textbook writers' cognition and agency are hauled in a push-and-pull dynamics where teachers' cognition and agency actually guide the reform process. Curricular reform, thus, follows the pull direction levered by teacher cognition and agency (see Fig. 6.1).** We, further, argue that this, then, guides all teaching which is **exam-centric** in nature.

As mentioned before, this study sheds light on the dissonance that exists between minority textbook writers' cognition that guided the conceptualisation, design and writing of the MIE government-endorsed textbooks and teacher cognition and agency. As the persons who have contributed to the vision underpinning the curricular reform as well as the conceptualisation, design and writing of the English Grades 7 to 9 English textbooks, the question remains whether we should put aside our own cognition and agency that governed the choices that we make when conceptualising, designing and writing a textbook and whether we should accept to work with teacher cognition and agency and their *colonial subjugated minds* and gear the writing of textbooks towards practice for exams. **As minority textbook writers, we find this highly problematic**

---

[3] Our emphasis.

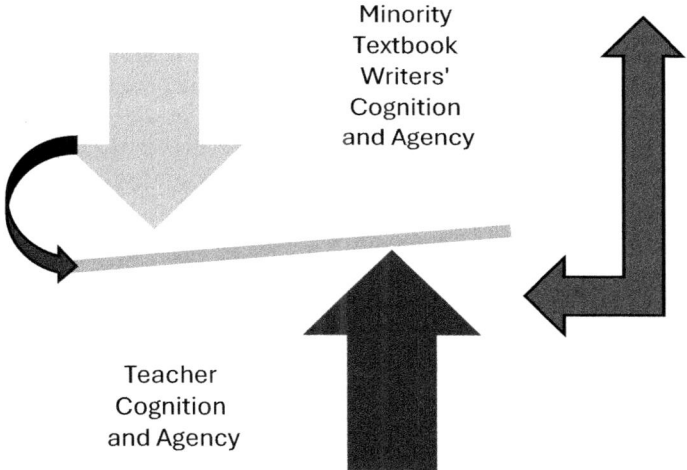

Fig. 6.1 Curricular reform and the pull direction

as it means giving up on our beliefs, our own philosophy, our cognition and, therefore, our agency. Although we are governed by numerous stakeholders and we are accountable to the government as well as to the teachers we empower and the teachers and students who are recipients of our textbooks, it is hard for us to put aside our own cognition and agency when it comes to teaching multilingual students in a SIDS country, like Mauritius.

Private supplementary teaching, or shadow education, has also exacerbated the divide between 'official textbooks' written by MIE, which are endorsed by the government, and those written privately, which are largely examination-based or grammar-oriented. Unlike private sector textbook writers who can choose to write "exams-friendly" or "consumer-friendly" textbooks for specific audiences because they are not accountable to policymakers, it is hard for us, as minority textbook writers, *also academics empowering teachers, to teach pedagogically at all levels,* to compromise on the **learner-centred curriculum** that we have developed on the basis that it might not be translated into the classroom. While these private sector textbooks respond to a wide demand on the part of teachers and parents, do they really cater to the learners' overall language development, or do they really prepare **all students** to sit for the end-of-year examinations? Indeed, this study has raised numerous questions for us as minority textbook writers and to us, *the dissonance between our own cognition and agency and those of the teachers come across as a dead-end*. Curricular reform is an inevitable and recurrent feature of the educational landscape. We, however, want to argue that curricular reform in almost all ex-colonies, including SIDS as Mauritius, meets with resistance as **teacher cognition and agency is shaped and moulded by the colonial subjugated mind.**[4] In the face of this, we can either bow down to the language of domination or stand up and speak to this cognition and agency by **claiming our own voices as minority textbook writers.**[5]

In our case, although we take into account the findings of this piece of research and will include it in future curricular reform, when it happens, it, nevertheless, does not mean that we will forego on our own cognition and agency. We cannot be minority textbook writers, commissioned by the government to lead the curricular reform and bring to it our vision shaped by **our own cognition and agency, which is infused with a decolonial stance and give up on what we feel, think and believe is soundly right for our children and the future of any curricular reform.**[6] We have, never, negated teacher cognition and agency and the reality in which teachers function locally and do not negate the importance that the colonial examination system has but **we strongly believe in the ethos that guides our own philosophy, our cognition and agency and want to end that any curricular reform should also strike the balance between minority textbook writers' cognition, agency and voice with that of the teachers' who are the drivers of the curricular reform.** If the teachers are the drivers of the curricular reform, as minority textbook writers, we are the fuel of this curricular reform, and the textbook is but one element of the curricular reform. We move on to **argue that a curricular reform is only possible when teaching and learning is aligned to meet one common aim, equipping the children with the requisite skills,**

---

[4] Our emphasis.
[5] Our emphasis.
[6] Our emphasis.

competencies and attitudes so that they can not only succeed in the exams but also develop in wholly and fully emotionally, mentally and physically adults who will function to their utmost best in the twenty-first century, translating our own vision at the heart of this curricular reform, as minority textbook writers, based in a SIDS (Small Islands Developing States) country.

References

Issit, J. (2004). Reflections on the study of textbooks. *History of Education, 33*(6), 683–696. https://doi.org/10.1080/0046760042000277834

Mauritius Examinations Syndicate (MES). (2020). *National Certificate of Education English Specimen Paper for first assessment in October 2020.* Mauritius Examinations Syndicate.

Concluding Thoughts

Although the findings of this study cannot be generalised, it can be claimed that the different participants; the teachers of our study, of whom only three had a Postgraduate Certificate in Education(PGCE) had strong teacher cognition and agency. Their teaching styles and learning preferences were deeply based on their beliefs and the contextual factors in which they were embedded. As mentioned before, this study pits forth the dissonance that exists between the principles that guided the conceptualisation, design and writing of the government-endorsed MIE textbooks and the usage of the textbooks by the teachers, who are guided only by their own cognition and agency. These teachers are resistant to the NYCBE reform and refuse to embrace the ethos and philosophy that guide the government-endorsed textbooks as they are exam-centric in nature. They use the textbooks accordingly then. As minority textbook writers who have contributed to the development and writing of the curriculum as well as the conceptualisation, design and writing of the English Grades 7 to 9 English textbooks, the question remains whether we should put aside the principles that govern the choices that we make when conceptualising, designing and writing a textbook and whether we should accept to work with the beliefs and expectations of teachers, and gear the writing of textbooks towards practice for exams. As minority textbook writers, our teaching and learning beliefs, values and principles are grounded in our conception of the NCF as well as the TLS TLS we conceived of, designed and wrote. We believe in the philosophy that underpinned the conceptualisation, designing and writing of the Grades 7-9 textbooks and therefore, it is always a push and pull dynamics that govern our own take and stance towards this curricular reform as well as the perspectives that govern the teacher's attitudes and stance taken towards the curricular reform.

Private supplementary teaching, or shadow education, has also exacerbated the divide between 'official textbooks' written at the MIE (Mauritius Institute of Education) and those written privately, which are, largely, examination-based or grammar-oriented. Unlike private sector textbook writers who can choose to write 'exams-friendly' or 'consumer-friendly' textbooks for specific audiences because they are not accountable to policymakers, it is hard for minority textbook writers, like us, to **compromise on the curriculum that we have developed on the basis that it might not be translated into the classroom.** This study has raised numerous questions for us as minority textbook writers and to us, the dissonance between our beliefs and realities and those of the teachers come across as a dead-end. While these private sector textbooks seem to be responding to a wide demand on the part of teachers and parents, do they cater to the learners' overall language aptitude, competencies, skills as well as their attitudes or do they only prepare them for exams? Already, some teachers have responded to this situation by integrating both types of textbooks into their practice. Hence, at the end of this study, it is believed that there should be more research which allows for a deeper understanding of how to design textbooks which align the minority textbook writers cognition and agency and that of the teachers, the engineers and the drivers of the curricular reform.

Curriculum Change and Teacher Agency

Curriculum change is an inevitable and continuous process in the education landscape, and like many other countries is very much linked to changes in political change and resulting policy changes. This process is often met with resistance, as teachers' agency and practices may not align with the newly introduced curriculum. While this has been the principal focus of this research, we cannot also ignore the implications of curriculum change for us, minority textbook writers designers who are, also, academics training teachers across all levels as we meet the same resistance in our classrooms, mostly.

Our study highlighted a dissonance between minority textbook writers' cognition and agency which guided the government-endorsed MIE textbooks and teachers' cognition and agency. While the textbooks aimed to promote communicative competence and learner-centred approaches, most teachers prioritise exam-oriented teaching and traditional grammar instruction. This disconnect underscores the importance of considering teacher perspectives and potential resistance when designing and implementing curriculum change.

As minority textbook writers who train teachers coming from different levels of schooling, we are always trying to strike a balance between our own cognition and agency and that of the teachers we work with. We understand their reality, whilst still maintaining our own take on education, teaching and learning. We are well grounded in our own teaching and learning philosophy, enough to strike a balance in our classroom, but unable to really push forward the curricular reform beyond our textbook writing and empowering our trainee teachers in our classroom. We, also, realised that by enacting curricular reform, policymakers and curriculum designers as well as minority textbook writers cannot expect rapid adoption unless all stakeholders believe in the curricular reform. The reform is bound to meet with resistance if the teachers are governed by their exam-centric teaching philosophy and they teach only to the exams and not towards the competencies, skills and attitudes laid out in the NCF as well as the TLS. When the exams itself is not aligned with the curricular reform, then as engineers of the curricular reform as well as minority textbook writers of the cogwheel that the textbook is in the car that the curricular reform is, we have only so much power at guiding the whole expanse of the NYCBE reform. Our role really stops at the conceptualisation, design and writing the textbooks as well as empowering our trainee teachers with the critical know how of the pedagogical choices that govern the use of a textbook, so they can be take and partake of the reform, either by enacting it or resisting it. Beyond this, teacher agency and cognition as well as the exams drive the curricular reform of Mauritius. Such is the case across the globe as well as a SIDS as Mauritius. Educational contexts might vary geographically but when it comes to curricular reform, teachers are the main drivers of any reform and geography changes nothing in it. Agency and cognition drive curricular reform and we can only aspire to a day when minority textbook writers stop being the subaltern they are due to the colonial mentality which drives most educational systems around the world, with exams being the engine of teacher agency and cognition.

REFERENCES

Ahmadi, E. (2012). Retrospective evaluation of textbook 'Summit 2B' for its suitability for EFL undergraduate students. *Journal of Educational and Social Research, 2*(5), 195–195.

Ahmadi, A., & Derakhshan, A. (2016). EFL teachers' perceptions towards textbook evaluation. *Theory and Practice in Language Studies, 6*(2), 260.

Ahour, T., Towhidiyan, B., & Saeidi, M. (2014). The evaluation of 'English Textbook 2' taught in Iranian high schools from teachers' Perspectives. *English Language Teaching, 7*(3), 150–158.

Appadoo-Ramsamy, W. (2022) *Teacher agency: A case study of Mauritius* (Doctoral dissertation).

Atkinson, D. (2021). The adaptive expertise of expert ELT textbook writers. *RELC Journal, 52*(3), 603–617.

Bakken, J., & Andersson-Bakken, E. (2021). The textbook task as a genre. *Journal of Curriculum Studies, 53*(6), 729–748. https://doi.org/10.1080/00220272.2021.1929499

Baleghizadeh, S., & Dargahi, Z. (2016). What aspects of creativity enhancement do ELT textbooks take into account? In *SLA research and materials development for language learning* (pp. 185–197). Routledge.

Bandura, A. (2006). Towards a psychology of human agency. *Perspectives on Psychological Science, 1*(2), 164–180. https://doi.org/10.1111/j.1745-6916.2006.00011.x

Birt, L., Scott, S., Cavers, D., Campbell, C., & Walter, F. (2016). Member checking: A tool to enhance trustworthiness or merely a nod to validation? *Qualitative Health Research, 26*(13), 1802–1811. https://doi.org/10.1177/1049732316654870

Bock, A. (2018). Chapter 4: Theories and methods of textbook studies. In E. Fuchs & A. Bock (Eds.), *The Palgrave handbook of textbook studies* (pp. 57–70). Palgrave Macmillan.

Bogdan, R., & Biklen, S. K. (1997). *Qualitative research for education*. Allyn & Bacon.

Borg, S. (2003). Teacher cognition in language teaching: A review of research on what language teachers think, know, believe, and do. *Language Teaching, 36*(2), 81–109.

Bunwaree, S. (1994). *Mauritian education in a global economy*. Editions de l'Océan Indien Ltée.

Carless, D. (2007). The suitability of task-based approaches for secondary schools: Perspectives from Hong Kong. *System, 35*(4), 595–608.

Carranza, C. P., & Cuayahuiltl, E. R. (2015). Influence of contextual factors on EFL Mexican teachers' beliefs and the use of textbooks. *How, 22*(2), 75–90.

Central Intelligence Agency. (2020). *The world factbook: Africa-Mauritius*. https://www.cia.gov/library/publications/the-world-factbook/geos/mp.html

Central Statistics Office. (2022). *Population census main results*. Retrieved January 20, 2025, from http://statsmauritius.govmu.org/Documents/Statistics/ESI/2022/EI1687/2022%20Population%20Census_Main%20Results_18112022.pdf

Charmaz, K., & Smith, J. (2003). Grounded theory. *Qualitative psychology: A practical guide to research methods, 2*, 81–110.

Chaudenson, R. (2006). A curiosity of Mauritian Creole. In K. J. Rottett, C. J. Clements, T. A. Klingler, & D. Piston-Hatlen (Eds.), *History, society and variation: In honor of Albert Valdman* (pp. 153–161). John Benjamins Publishing Company.

Cochran-Smith, M., & Lytle, S. L. (1999). Relationships of knowledge and practice: Teacher learning in communities. *Review of Research in Education, 24*(1), 249–305.

Collen, L. (2016). Mauritian Kreol confronts English and French Hydras. In P. Bunce, R. Phillipson, V. Rapatahana, & R. Tupas (Eds.), *Why English? Confronting the hydra* (pp. 159–170). Multilingual Matters.

Colony of Mauritius. The Education ordinance. (1957). *A collection of ordinances proclamations and government notices published during the year 1957*. (1958). Port Louis, Mauritius: J. Eliel Felix, I.S.O., Government printer.

Craig, C. J. (2009). Research in the midst of organized school reform: Versions of teacher community in tension. *American Educational Research Journal*, *46*(2), 598–619. https://doi.org/10.3102/0002831208330213

Creswell, J. W. (2002). *Educational research: Planning, conducting, and evaluating quantitative research* (Vol. 7). Prentice Hall.

Creswell, J. W. (2005). *Educational research: Planning, conducting, and evaluating quantitative and qualitative research* (2nd ed.). Pearson Education.

Creswell, J. W., & Poth, C. N. (2016). *Qualitative inquiry and research design: Choosing among five approaches*. Sage Publications.

Das, V. (2023). Subaltern as perspective. In D. Brydon (Ed.), *Postcolonialism: Critical concepts* (pp. 1478–1490). Routledge.

Datnow, A. (2020). The role of teachers in educational reform: A 20-year perspective. *Journal of Educational Change*, *21*(3), 431–441.

DeLyser, D., Herbert, S., Aitken, S., Crang, M., & McDowell, L. (2010). *The SAGE handbook of qualitative geography*. SAGE Publications.

Denzin, N. K. (2012). Triangulation 2.0. *Journal of Mixed Methods Research*, *6*(2), 80–88.

Ebrahimi, F., & Sahragard, R. (2017). Teachers' perceptions of the new English textbooks in Iranian junior high schools. *Journal of Asia TEFL*, *14*(2), 355.

Finlay, L. (2002). 'Outing' the researcher: The provenance, process, and practice of reflexivity. *Qualitative Health Research*, *12*(4), 531–545. https://doi.org/10.1177/104973202129120052

Ghorbani, M. R. (2011). Quantification and graphic representation of EFL textbook evaluation results. *Theory and Practice in Language Studies*, *1*(5), 511–520.

Gramsci, A. (1971). *Selections from the prison notebooks* (Q. Hoare & G. N. Smith, Ed. and Trans.). International Publishers

Hammersley, M., & Traianou, A. (2012). *Ethics in qualitative research: Controversies and contexts*. SAGE Publications.

Haß, F. (Ed.). (2006). *Fachdidaktik Englisch: Tradition Innovation Praxis*. Klett.

Hornby, A. S., Wehmeier, S., & Ashby, M. (Eds.). (2000). *Oxford advanced learner's dictionary of current English* (6th ed.). Oxford University Press.

Huang, R., Tlili, A., Zhang, X., Sun, T., Wang, J., Sharma, R. C., & Burgos, D. (2022). A Comprehensive framework for comparing textbooks: Insights from the literature and experts. *Sustainability*, *14*(11), 6940.

Humes, W., & Priestley, M. (2021). Curriculum reform in Scottish education: Discourse, narrative and enactment. In *Curriculum making in Europe: Policy and practice within and across diverse contexts* (pp. 175–198). Emerald Publishing Limited.

Issit, J. (2004). Reflections on the study of textbooks. *History of Education*, *33*(6), 683–696. https://doi.org/10.1080/0046760042000277834

Janko, T., & Pešková, K. (2017). Exploring teachers' perceptions of curriculum change and their use of textbooks during its implementation: A review of current research. *Zeitschrift für Geographiedidaktik | Journal of Geography Education, 45*(1), 33–60. https://doi.org/10.18452/23097

Jawaheer, M. (2019). Trainee teachers' perceptions towards using constructivist pedagogy to foster deep learning approaches to the study of literature at lower secondary. In W. Zoghbor, S. Al Alami, & T. Alexiou (Eds.), *Proceedings of the 1st Applied Linguistics and Language Teaching (ALLT) Conference*, p. 144.

Jawaheer, M. (2022). Introducing ecopoetry in teacher education to promote sustainable education at lower secondary level in Mauritius. In *Management and leadership for a sustainable Africa, Volume 3: Educating for sustainability outcomes* (pp. 65–85). Springer International Publishing.

Jinot, B. L. (2017). A critical review of the current education system of Mauritius and the learner discipline problem in Mauritian state secondary schools. *Journal of Education and Social Sciences, 8*(1), 47–55.

Johnsen, E. B. (1993). *Textbooks in the kaleidoscope*. Oxford University Press.

Khan, K., Khan, W., Hayat, Y., Ahmad, S. M., & Raza, K. K. (2020). A comparative study of students' and teachers' perceptions about English textbooks at intermediate level and their role in promoting students' proficiency in English. *International Journal of English Linguistics, 10*(2), 40–50.

Khan, A., Rafique, S., & Khalid, S. (2024). Evaluation of the Federal English textbook of Grade One of Federal schools in Pakistan. *Journal of Applied Linguistics and TESOL (JALT), 7*(4), 70–84.

Kim, J. (2024). Why do teachers not change while the national curriculum repeatedly changes?: The 'hidden' resistance of teachers in the centralized system of education in South Korea. *International Journal of Educational Development, 109*, 103105.

Kong, J. E., & Sung, K. (2021). English teachers' views on culture teaching through analyzing cultural background in middle school English textbooks. *Studies in Foreign Language Education, 35*(3), 167–190.

Korlapu-Bungaree, R. (2020). *English literature teachers' pedagogical choices at upper secondary level: Narratives of Mauritian teachers* (Doctoral dissertation).

Kumar, K. (2023). *Textbooks and the curriculum: Understanding the politics*. https://www.thehinducentre.com/the-arena/67053469-Textbooks-and-the-Curriculum-Understanding-the-Politics.pdf

Kumaravadivelu, B. (2006). *Understanding language teaching: From method to postmethod*. Routledge.

Latif, A., & Mahmoud, M. M. (2012). Teaching a standard-based communicative English textbook series to secondary school students in Egypt: Investigating teachers' practices and beliefs. *English teaching: Practice and critique, 11*(3), 78–97.

Lee, R. N., & Bathmaker, A. M. (2007). The use of English textbooks for teaching English to vocational students in Singapore secondary schools: A survey of teachers' Beliefs. *RELC journal, 38*(3), 350–374.

Li, S. C., Poon, A. Y., Lai, T. K., & Tam, S. T. (2021). Does middle leadership matter? Evidence from a study of system-wide reform on English language curriculum. *International Journal of Leadership in Education, 24*(2), 226–243.

Lincoln, Y. S., & Guba, E. G. (1985). *Naturalistic inquiry.* Sage.

Mahadeo, S. K. (2006). English language teaching in Mauritius: A need for clarity of vision regarding English language policy. *The International Journal of Language, Society and Culture, 18*, 18–12.

Mahboob, A., & Elyas, T. (2014). English in the kingdom of Saudi Arabia. *World Englishes, 33*(1), 128–142.

Mauritius Examinations Syndicate (MES). (2015). *Mauritius—National assessment at Form III.* Retrieved June 12, 2024, from http://nada.uis.unesco.org/nada/en/index.php/catalogue/175

Mauritius Examinations Syndicate (MES). (2020). *National Certificate of Education English Specimen Paper for first assessment in October 2020.* Mauritius Examinations Syndicate.

Mauritius Institute of Education. (2017). *National curriculum framework—Nine year continuous basic education Grades 7, 8 & 9.* Mauritius Institute of Education.

Mauritius Institute of Education. (2018). *Curriculum.* Retrieved January 21, 2024, from https://portal.mie.ac.mu/curriculum-development/

Mauritius Institute of Education. (2021). *Grade 7 English language: A fun learning experience.* Ministry of Education, Tertiary Education, Science & Technology.

Merseth, K. K. (1996). Cases and case methods in teacher education. In J. Sikula (Ed.), *Handbook of research on teacher education* (2nd ed., pp. 722–744). Macmillan.

MIE. (2019–2020). *Annual report 2019–2020 empowering professionals for quality education.*

Miles, W. F. S. (2000). The politics of language equilibrium in a multilingual society: Mauritius. *Comparative Politics, 32*(2), 215–230.

Ministry of Education and Human Resources Tertiary and Scientific Research. (2009). *NCF 2009.*

Ministry of Education and Human Resources Tertiary and Scientific Research. (2016). *Nine years of continuous basic education: Inspiring every child.* Retrieved February 13, 2024, from http://ministry-education.govmu.org/English/educationsector/nys/Documents/NYCBEBooklet.pdf

Ministry of Education and Human Resources, Tertiary Education and Scientific Research. (2017). *Explaining the NYCBE Reform-The Secondary Sector.* Ministry of Education and Human Resources, Tertiary Education and Scientific Research.

Mitchell, B., & Buntic, C. G. (2023). Global trends in curriculum reform and development. *Curriculum and Teaching, 38*(1), 27–47.

Nunan, D. (1999). *Second language teaching & learning*. Heinle & Heinle Publishers.

Oates, T. (2014). *Why textbooks count a policy paper*. University of Cambridge, Local Examinations Syndicate..

Okoth, T. A. (2016). Challenges of implementing a top-down curriculum innovation in English language teaching: Perspectives of form Iii English language teachers in Kenya. *Journal of Education and Practice, 7*(3), 169–177.

Panezai, S. G., & Channa, L. A. (2017). Pakistani government primary school teachers and the English textbooks of Grades 1–5: A mixed methods teachers'-led evaluation. *Cogent Education, 4*(1), 1269712.

Parlindungan, F., Rifai, I., & Safriani, A. (2018). The representation of Indonesian cultural diversity in middle school English textbooks. *Indonesian Journal of Applied Linguistics, 8*(2), 289–302.

Pavlenko, V. (2021). Textbook as a means of creativity development of a student. *Українська полоністика, 19*, 126–133.

Raees, C. (2018). Policies, textbooks, and curriculum constraints to integrating literature into language education: EFL teacher perspectives from Russia. *Pedagogika, 132*(4), 178–196.

Rahimi, M., & Hassani, M. (2012). Attitude towards EFL textbooks as a predictor of attitude towards learning English as a foreign language. *Procedia-Social and Behavioral Sciences, 1*(31), 66–72.

Rahman, M. M., Johan, M., Selim, S. M. M., Singh, M. K. M., & Shahed, F. H. (2019). Teachers' beliefs and practices of implementing secondary English curriculum reform in Bangladesh: A phenomenological study. *Journal of Asia TEFL, 16*(2), 591.

Ravitch, S. M., & Carl, N. M. (2021). *Qualitative research: Bridging the conceptual, theoretical, and methodological* (2nd ed.). SAGE Publications.

Reeves, T. C., & Hedberg, J. G. (2002). *Interactive learning systems evaluation*. Educational Technology Publications.

Rosyida, E. M. R. (2016). Teachers' perceptions toward the use of English textbook. *English Education: Jurnal Tadris Bahasa Inggris, 9*(1), 43–54.

Rughoonundun-Chellapermal, N. (2017). Autopsie de l'échec d'un projet d'éducation multilingue. *Cahiers internationaux de sociolinguistique, 2*, 155–177.

Sahlberg, P. (2021). *Finnish lessons 3.0: What can the world learn from educational change in Finland?* Teachers College Press.

Schwab, K. (2019). *The global competitiveness report 2019*. Retrieved September 30, 2024, from http://www3.weforum.org/docs/WEF_TheGlobalCompetitivenessReport2019.pdf

Sonck, G. (2005). Language of instruction and instructed languages in Mauritius. *Journal of Multilingual and Multicultural Development, 26*(1), 37–51.

Srakang, L. (2013). *A study of teachers perceptions toward using English textbooks: A case study of 10th grade English teachers in Maha Sarakham Province* (Doctoral dissertation).

Stake, R. E. (1995). *The art of case study research.* SAGE Publications.

Stake, R. E. (2006). *Multiple case study analysis.* The Guilford Press.

Strauss, A., & Corbin, J. (1998). *Basics of qualitative research: techniques and procedures for developing grounded theory* (2nd ed.). SAGE.

Tirvassen, R. (1998). *Langues, éducation et développement: le cas de l'Île Maurice.* Aix-Marseille 1.

Tosun, S. (2013). A comparative study on evaluation of Turkish and English foreign language textbooks. *Procedia-Social and Behavioral Sciences, 70,* 1374–1380.

Tran, N. G., Ha, X. V., & Tran, N. H. (2023). EFL reformed curriculum in Vietnam: An understanding of teachers' cognitions and classroom practices. *RELC Journal, 54*(1), 166–182.

Underwood, P. R. (2012). Teacher beliefs and intentions regarding the instruction of English grammar under national curriculum reforms: A Theory of Planned Behaviour perspective. *Teaching and Teacher Education, 28*(6), 911–925.

Van Steen, M. S. J. (2019). *Attitudes towards learning english as a second language in primary schools in Mauritius* (Master's thesis).

Wa Thiong'o, N. (1998). Decolonising the mind. *Diogenes, 46*(184), 101–104.

Waldis, B. (2003). *Styles of multiculturalism in Mauritius: A case study in education policy.* https://books.google.mu/books?id=X9OMDwAAQBAJ&pg=PA71&lpg=PA71&dq=education+ordinance+mauritius&source=bl&ots=fmWNwILmrf&sig=ACfU3U0f2GyB7f8IXO46h4RuNefyZjspiA&hl=en&sa=X&ved=2ahUKEwj06ZL08NLnAhVDMewKHc3QDhs4ChDoATAEegQIDBAB#v=onepage&q&f=false

Wallace, C. S., & Priestley, M. (2011). Teacher beliefs and the mediation of curriculum innovation in Scotland: A socio-cultural perspective on professional development and change. *Journal of Curriculum Studies, 43*(3), 357–381.

Wan Khin, E. K. M. (2023). *Children's voice in investigating their use of multilingual abilities in learning to read in two or more languages in the Mauritian context* (Doctoral dissertation, University of Brighton).

Wen-Cheng, W., Chien-Hung, L., & Chung-Chieh, L. (2011). Thinking of the textbook in the ESL/EFL classroom. *English Language Teaching, 4*(2), 91–96.

Yin, R. K. (2014). *Case study research: Design and methods* (5th ed.). SAGE Publications.

Index

A
Additional resources, 45, 47, 77, 80

B
Beliefs, 18, 20–22, 28, 29, 49, 50, 60, 68–70, 77, 78, 88

C
Case studies, 28
Change agents, 9
Classroom observations, 38
Collaborative, 30, 36, 37
Collaborative analysis, 37
Competencies, 16, 20, 21, 43, 45, 46, 49, 50, 76, 86
Credibility, 36, 37
Cross-case analysis, 36
Curriculum coherence, 8
Curriculum materials, 29
Curriculum reform, 14, 18, 22, 72

D
Dissonance, 85, 88, 93, 95
Document analysis, 32, 38

E
English Language Teaching (ELT), 16, 20
Exam-oriented, *see* Exams
Exam practice, 22
  See also Exams
Exams, 31, 42–46, 49–51, 57–59, 70, 76, 80, 82, 86, 88, 93

F
Freedom, 72

G
Grounded theory, 30, 36

I
In-depth interviews, 38
Interpretivism, 28
　See also Qualitative research

L
Learner-centred, 14

N
National Curriculum Framework (NCF), 17, 63, 78, 86

O
Opposition, 15

P
Pedagogical choices, 2, 9, 33, 34, 36, 41, 42, 44, 49, 50, 56, 59, 60, 69, 71, 72, 78, 80, 82, 88
Perceptions, 2, 10, 19–21, 23, 31, 33, 36, 41, 42, 56, 58, 71, 72, 76
Private sector textbook writers, 89, 94
Private supplementary teaching, 89, 94
Professional development, 19, 22

Q
Qualitative research, 28, 29

R
Reflexivity, 36
Reliability, 36
Representation, 41
Resistance, 15

S
Shadow education, 89, 94
　See also Private supplementary teaching
Subaltern, 9

T
Teacher agency, vii, 21, 22, 29, 42, 50, 70, 77, 82, 88
Teachers' cognition, 18
Teaching of grammar, 43–44, 50, 73, 77
Trustworthiness, 37

GPSR Compliance

The European Union's (EU) General Product Safety Regulation (GPSR) is a set of rules that requires consumer products to be safe and our obligations to ensure this.

If you have any concerns about our products, you can contact us on ProductSafety@springernature.com

In case Publisher is established outside the EU, the EU authorized representative is:

Springer Nature Customer Service Center GmbH
Europaplatz 3
69115 Heidelberg, Germany

Batch number: 09457624

Printed by Printforce, the Netherlands